THE FULL MONTY

This book is to be returned on or before
the last date stamped below.

Learning Services
City of Westminster College
Maida Vale Centre
London W9 2NR
0171 258 2829

The Full Monty

Simon Beaufoy

SCREENPRESS BOOKS

First published in 1997
by ScreenPress Books
28 Castle Street Eye Suffolk IP23 7AW

Photoset by Parker Typesetting Service, Leicester
Printed in England by Clays Ltd, St Ives plc

A CIP record for this book
is available from the British Library

ISBN 1–901680–02–9

For more information on forthcoming ScreenPress Books
please contact the publishers at:

ScreenPress Books 28 Castle Street
Eye Suffolk
IP23 7AW
or fax on: 01379 870 261

2 4 6 8 10 9 7 5 3 1

To Sheffield, a wonderful city,
and to Rod, with thanks

Peter Cattaneo

FOREWORD

In the midst of the usual trials and tribulations of making a film,
– exhaustion, self-doubt, paranoia, insomnia, general
personality and sanity breakdown, – I tried always to keep one
thing in mind, how I felt when I first read Simon's script. From
the beginning, I was completely wrapped up in the story and
the characters, quietly moved one minute, laughing out loud the
next.

Whilst being a very simple tale, the journey Simon takes us
on is full of unexpected turns and delightful characterisation.
The characters are real, distinctive and drawn with great warmth
and affection. Each member of the gang makes an unforgettable
entrance, from Guy throwing himself at the wall to Lomper's
failed suicide, and their personalities are swiftly and engagingly
defined. Even some of the more apparently improvised
character details in the film, such as when Dave gets the blue
plastic ring stuck on his wrist, are here in the original script.

Issues of male identity, gender roles, body politics and the
effects of long-term unemployment are dealt with but without
the script ever becoming didactic. These themes are always
present but never at the expense of character or story. A great
sense of irony keeps the spirit light and makes sure the film
never takes itself too seriously – even in its darkest moments.
Never is this more apparent than in the scene where Gaz and
Dave bring Lomper round from the brink of suicide. Writing
like this gives the cast everything they need to work with, –
irony, character, tenderness, – and leaves a director (certainly
this one) with the easiest job.

Finally, mention should be made of the film's producer,
Uberto Pasolini. He was the originator of the project, an
insightful, and energetic script editor and remained a huge
creative influence, to the very last cut of the film.

Peter Cattaneo, 1997

Simon Beaufoy

INTRODUCTION

Some years ago I spent a lot of time in Sheffield visiting a girlfriend in hospital. In between visiting hours, I would wander the streets with the slow tread of those who have nowhere to go and a lot of time in which to get there. After a while I began to notice that I wasn't the only one moonwalking around Sheffield's parks, streets and shops, trying to dredge up some enthusiasm for a Dixons mid-season sale. There were thousands of us, nearly all men, On the Wander.

Even the wanderers with dogs didn't behave like dog-walkers. Where was the chirrup of praise at the fouled playing field? The rewarding pat as another child was dispatched to hospital? Animal was as depressed as man, and a thrown stick would result merely in owner and dog looking dolefully at each other, as if acknowledging the utter pointlessness of stick-throwing in a godless universe.

And sharing companionable silences with these wanderers under the bandstand in the park as the rain came down, I got to thinking. Where were all the women? It appeared that, unlike the men, the women had jobs. Not perhaps good jobs: cashier, packing, shelf-stacking jobs in the monstrous Meadowhall Shopping Centre that replaced the steel-rolling mills. But jobs nevertheless. Which meant money. Which meant Friday nights down the pub with the . . . well, it used to be lads. But the lads were out walking their invisible dogs, wondering why people didn't want steel any more, just shopping centres.

When, a few years later, Uberto Pasolini, the producer suggested a film about unemployed men becoming male strippers, all sorts of things clicked into place. Strange role-reversals were going on all around us. Men stripping, not women. Women going out to work, not men . . . Suddenly, it seemed, women had money in their pockets: money that bought independence and a desire to even out a few little discrepancies between men and women. Two thousand years of servitude, for instance. Women began to look at men in the same way that men had been looking at women – and new cars – for generations. And it wasn't a pretty sight. Which is where the male strippers come in. Literally and metaphorically men were being told to shape up, get fit, get smart and get sexy. I can't think of a better way to sum up the socio-political gender shifts of the late twentieth century than to ask you this: ten years ago, would you, as a man, have given the purchase of a new pair of underpants a second thought? Or even a first thought? Five years ago, would you have weighed up Calvin Klein thoughtfully against Jockey and finally forked out twenty-eight quid for a *pair of pants?* The days of the battle-scarred grunty had gone forever.

But there are a lot of puzzled-looking blokes left behind by this new world order. *The Full Monty* is a tribute to all those men who are trying, manfully, to catch up.

Simon Beaufoy
1997

THE FULL MONTY

TITLE SEQUENCE

Distressed black and white film stock. Controlled by men in baggy 1950s overalls and caps, a stream of molten ore is being poured into pig-iron moulds. Sparks fly in the huge rolling mill. A clipped English accent accompanies the pictures.

MAN
(*voice-over*)
Sheffield: the beating heart of the industrial North. Never have men been so busy, working day and night to make the steel that is fuelling the recovery of our nation . . .

A wide shot shows the entire Sheffield Basin – mile upon mile of working steel mills. As the voice-over gradually fades, the picture mixes into a shot of the Basin as it is today – a desolate landscape only partially filled by a shopping centre with a gargantuan, empty car park. In place of the thump of machinery is the empty ring of a distant burglar alarm. Tiny in the frame, a Man and a Boy stand on a motorway footbridge staring at the view. A Roller-blader speeds from one side of the frame to the other and away. The Man glances after him in disgust, throws his cigarette onto the ground. The Man and Boy both turn and walk away.

EXT. SHEFFIELD. DAY

A fine rain blankets the council estate. From somewhere can be heard the noise of a hoover and a man singing in a confidently tuneless Yorkshire accent. Through the drizzle the Man and the Boy can be seen crouched behind a wall watching Jean, a sturdy woman in her mid-thirties. She walks

3

out of a council house, remembers something and shouts up at the open bedroom window from where the sound of hoovering is coming.

JEAN

Dave love? Dave!

No response. Jean gives up and walks off down the road.

INT./EXT. DAVE'S HOUSE. DAY

A barrel-chested goliath in his mid-thirties is giving the upstairs bedroom an incongruously dainty hoover. With a flowery pinafore stretched across his impressive stomach, Dave hoovers up what looks like a pebble that has appeared on the carpet. He turns only to find that another, larger one has appeared. Assiduously he vacuums this one up too. It rattles alarmingly into the hoover. A third pebble comes through the window, unseen by Dave until it lands. Becoming perplexed, Dave picks up this one, stops singing, takes off his glasses, shakes the hoover, attributes it to one of nature's mysteries and carries on. Then a cowboy boot flies through the window and hits the opposite wall with a smack. Dave finally clicks and goes to the window.

Outside, amidst the remnants of a Ford Granada that constitute Dave's front garden, the Man and the Boy have come out of hiding: Gaz, a thirty-year-old magnet for trouble and Nathan, his son, who at nine years old is the more mature of the two. Hunched in his ex-army parka, Gaz stands miserably on one leg using Nathan as a crutch.

GAZ

I'll put a grenade through next time, yer deaf bastard.

DAVE

I were hoovering, weren't I? Alright, Nathan, long time no see, eh?

NATHAN

Alright, Dave.

GAZ

I need an hand.

DAVE

Can't, Gaz. Told you, I'm 'oovering.

GAZ

You'll be staying in to wash your hair next, you. Come on, Dave mate, there's a pint in it.

DAVE
(*after a brief pause*)
Aye, alright then. If you're quick. Hang on.

Dave disappears from the window. The rain drips from Nathan's nose.

NATHAN
(*miserable*)
Chart Show's on in ten minutes.

GAZ

Ah, it's crap is that, Nath. You don't want to be watching that bollocks.

Dave reappears in the window again waving a letter.

DAVE

Here, Gaz, you seen this? 'Dear Mr Horsfall, you are invited to attend the Job Club.' That's not bad is it? I mean, personal invite, like –

GAZ

– we're all going.

DAVE

What, all of us?

GAZ

Yes.

DAVE
(*disappointed*)
Oh. I thought it were just me. Never been a member of a club before, have I? You sure?

Gaz finally loses his patience and pulls his hood down.

GAZ
Dave, are you gonna play the prince in the chuffin' tower all day, or what? It's raining out here.

DAVE
Alright, alright. Wait on, Job Seekers, I'm there.

EXT. DAVE'S HOUSE. DAY

Dave joins Gaz and Nathan on the road outside the house. He is carrying a pack of Jacob's Cream Crackers. He offers them around with his usual undaunted cheerfulness. Neither Gaz nor Nathan bother even to take their hands out of their pockets.

DAVE
Cream cracker, anybody?

GAZ
What you doing with *them*?

DAVE
On a diet, aren't I? You get used to 'em. You do. Well come on then.

Gaz gives Dave a look of pained patience.

GAZ
David.

> DAVE
> (*returning the pained patience*)
Garrold?

Gaz points to his feet, one of which is bootless.

Oh aye, sorry.

Dave trundles back inside.

INT. STEELWORKS. DAY

The quarter-mile-long rolling mill is deserted and crumbling. Hulks of machinery stand rusting in pools of water, dinosaurs from the days of heavy industry. Gaz and Dave are carting some lengths of ornate cast-iron drainpipe along the gantry of the rolling mill. They stumble along above the steelworks' huge cauldron – now long cold.

> GAZ
> (*whispering*)
You used to melt your boots up 'ere, it were that hot. Now look.

> NATHAN
Everyone else watches it. I never see it.

> GAZ
Oh shut up about the bloody *Chart Show*.

> DAVE
Shh. Listen.

The three stop.

> GAZ
What now?

> DAVE
Music.

NATHAN
(*brightening for the first time*)
Yeah?

GAZ
Dave, don't start him off.

DAVE
No listen.

Faintly they can hear an insistent, rhythmic thumping. Slowly it gets louder, more menacing. Gaz, Dave and Nathan look at each other, panic-struck.

What the hellfire's that?

NATHAN
Dad?

Way down the rolling mill, a phalanx of uniformed men swing into view, marching straight towards them.

GAZ
It's the Charge of the fucking Light Brigade.

DAVE
(*panicking*)
Hey now come on, we've only nicked some fuckin' pipes . . .

Gaz looks for somewhere to hide. Spotting the cauldron, he leaps in and helps Nathan down. Dave piles in after them. As the army of men get nearer, the final sounds of a marching tune echo around the walls. With the works' banner unfurled, the Steelworks Brass Band marches right underneath the cauldron with only the doleful beat of the bass drum to keep them marching. At the entrance to the rolling mill they put down their instruments, get out the roll-ups and disappear into the rain. Peering over the edge of the cauldron the three watch the band go.

                              GAZ
    Well you wanted music.

Nathan pulls a face at Gaz.

                              DAVE
                      (*embarrassed laugh*)
    'Course, I knew they were the works' band, like . . . Ey
    up, Security Penguin's back.

*One of the cornet players breaks from the band formation
and runs back to the rolling mill entrance. This is Lomper: tall
and skinny. Lomper gets into his car parked inside the mill,
drives it out and then shuts the big gate behind him. Gaz,
Nathan and Dave are locked in. Dave crunches a cream
cracker pointedly.*

                              GAZ
    Lompy little bastard.

                              DAVE
    Won't take a minute, he said, won't take a minute. Now
    what?

                              GAZ
    Shut up, I'm thinking.

                            NATHAN
                         (*to Dave*)
    Don't hold your breath.

EXT. CANAL. DAY

*Dave and Gaz stand precariously on a long-abandoned car
half sunk in the middle of the canal that runs along the edge
of the steel mill. One end of the stolen drainpipe is resting on
the car's roof, the other end reaches the far bank. Gaz is
supporting the pip while Nathan edges unhappily along it, just
above the dirty water, balancing another length of pipe in his
hands.*

GAZ

Told you. Did it in army, didn't we? Initiative tests.
Getting squaddies over shark-infested custard an' that.
Go on, kid.

NATHAN

Can't we do normal things sometimes?

GAZ

What's up with you? This is normal. Isn't it, Dave?

DAVE

Oh aye, everyday stuff, this. I think this bugger's
sinking.

Nathan gets to the other side.

GAZ

Nice one, Nath. How leg it home with that 'un.

NATHAN

Dad . . . What if I get caught? It's stealing.

GAZ

Liberating, love, liberating. Anyroad, you don't get a
criminal record 'til you're sixteen. You got years yet. Just
don't tell your mum.

*Nathan tries to pull the heavy pipe onto the bank. Inevitably,
he can't hold onto it and the pipe drops into the canal.*

You're useless, you. They're twenty quid each, them.
That were your bloody maintenance, were that.

Upset, Nathan trudges off down the towpath.

DAVE
(*to Gaz*)

Nice one.

GAZ

Nathan, Nathan . . .

Nathan stops and sits morosely on a dilapidated wall. Dave starts to move towards the pipe on the roof of the car.

With the shift of Dave's weight, the car lurches dramatically, almost throwing Dave into the water. Gaz hurls himself forward as Dave scrambles back and the car swings violently the other way. The pipe rolls off the car and disappears into the water.

GAZ

Stay still!

Dave freezes and Gaz creeps backwards. The car gently swings back to a horizontal position. Frozen in motion, Gaz and Dave are like panic-struck statues. They glare helplessly at each other.

DAVE

What's your 'initiative' got to say about this, then, bog-eyes?

GAZ
(after a bit more statue practice)
Ey up, someone coming.

A Dog-walker approaches along the tow-path. This being Yorkshire, he expresses no surprise at all.

DOG WALKER

Alright?

GAZ

Aye, not-so-bad.

Without breaking step, the Dog-walker disappears. Dave is incredulous.

DAVE
'Not-so-bad'? *'Not-so-bad'?* Not much of a fuckin' SOS, that, is it?

GAZ

Alright, alright, don't get a benny on, you'll have us both in. All we have to do is get the pipe –

DAVE

– what sodding pipe?

Gaz looks down and is struck dumb. The pipe has gone.

GAZ

Oh shit.
                    (*giggles*)
How's your breaststroke, Dave?

DAVE
                    (*heartfelt*)
You shag-bucket.

EXT. SHEFFIELD STREET. EVENING

Sodden from the waist down, Dave is squidging blackly along the street. Dry, Gaz follows behind, getting into his sweatshirt and parka. Nathan brings up the rear.

GAZ

It weren't that cold, were it?
                    (*no reply*)
Considering.
                    (*no reply*)
You should have taken your kit off, shouldn't you? What's up, you shy?

DAVE
                    (*turning sharply*)
Don't. Just shut up, alright?

They squidge along in silence. Dave pulls out the limpest packet of cream crackers and tries to rescue one, before throwing the whole lot away. A Young Woman comes towards them.

Aye up, Dave. Alright, darling?

The Young Woman stalks past, ignoring him. Gaz turns and walks backwards, watching her go.

What do you reckon? Six, maybe seven. Depends.
(*thoughtful*)
You can never see their knockers in winter, can you?

NATHAN

Dad . . .

They turn the corner and are confronted with hundreds of women queueing outside the working men's club.

GAZ

Happy Christmas . . .

NATHAN

It's them Chippendale efforts.

GAZ

You what?

NATHAN

Them dancers. Mum were going on about it.

GAZ

You're jesting me. She must be getting desperate.

They squidge past the giggling women.

You all waiting for me?

WOMAN

Yeah. To go home.

GAZ
(*undaunted*)
Well you know where to find me when you're tired of looking at them poofs.

DAVE

Come on, Gaz, I'm freezin'.

Dave stops by a poster to take off one of his trainers.

GAZ
(*reading*)
'Women only . . .' Cheeky benders. It's a bloody
working men's club, ta for asking. Look at him. Don't
know what you've got to smile about. I mean he's got no
willy for starters, has he?
(*tapping the poster on the appropriate part*)
There's nowt in a gym'll help you there, mate

*Dave is wringing out his sock. He gives it a quick sniff and
proceeds to put it back on. They set off walking again. Gaz
feels his biceps and, copying the poster, puffs up his chest
experimentally.*

Nah. No decent woman'd be seen dead in there.

DAVE
(*after a shifty pause*)
Jean would.

GAZ
(*stopping*)
Nay Dave . . . what's going on, mate?

DAVE
(*shrugs*)
It's her money, innit?

GAZ
Stripe me, Dave, you gonna just stand there whiles some
woofter is waving his tackle at your missus? You wanna
put your foot down, you do.

16

DAVE
(*missing the point*)
Me foot's soaking.

GAZ
Never mind that. Where's your pride, man? She's already
got you hoovering. I saw it and I let it go. But this . . .
no way, Dave. You wanna get her out of there and tell
her what for.

NATHAN
Can't. It's women only.

GAZ
Not through the bog window it's not. Now come on.

INT. TOILET. NIGHT

*Nathan drops to the floor of the gents' toilets followed by
Gaz. From outside the window comes Dave's voice.*

DAVE
(*off-screen*)
Just hurry up, will you? Me toes have gone numb.

GAZ
(*whispering*)
That's gratitude for you. We're riding into' Alley of
Death for you, you fat git.

DAVE
(*off-screen*)
It's not my fault I can't fit, is it?

GAZ
(*to Nathan*)
Go on, then. I'll be waiting here, keeping guard. Just
find Auntie Jean and tell her Uncle Dave wants a word
outside, alright?

NATHAN
Dad . . . Do I have to?

GAZ
Good lad, go on.

Nathan, reluctant, is pushed through the door. Peering through a tiny crack in the door, Gaz is confronted with hundreds of women all screaming, shouting and applauding, though at what, Gaz cannot see. He watches Nathan approach an empty bar table at the back of the hall and very deliberately pick up a half-empty bottle of beer and drain it. He moves swiftly onto a Pernod and black and then a whisky.

(*hissing*)
Nath! Nathan.

Gaz spots a group coming his way, slams the door and nips into one of the cubicles and peers through the hole left by the torn-off lock. The door bangs open and two drunken women stumble in, giggling: Sharon and Jean, Dave's wife, way over-dressed, in their mid-thirties.

JEAN
Well I'm not waiting in that queue.

SHARON
(*peering around*)
Ooh, I've allus wanted a nosey in men's bogs.

Bee, a leather and chain-clad Sheffield diva, who underneath the make-up could well be in her forties, crashes in after them.

BEE
Phoor, those bloody muscles . . . where'd he get 'em from, though? Tell you, you couldn't buy a bum like that round here.

Sharon and Jean park themselves in the cubicles next to a panic-stricken Gaz while Bee sorts out her make-up in the mirror.

JEAN

It's not their bodies, Bee, it's what they do with 'em . . . I can't remember the last time me and Dave got down to it.

SHARON

Don't know what you're moaning about with you-know-who on your tail.

BEE
(singing the 1960s number)
Frankieee . . .

JEAN

Listen, Frank doesn't fancy me and I don't fancy him, alright, so bloody give over.

Bee and Sharon pull a face and fall quiet. An evil smile appears on Jean's face.

Do you think he might though?

Both women roar their approval. Jean gets defensive again.

Well at least Franko talks to me.

SHARON

Oh he talks alright. It's when he starts juggling that you know you're in trouble.

BEE

Hell aye, remember when I were on pharmaceutical section with him? He comes up to us juggling three tubes of KY Jelly and a variety pack of condoms. Now that's what I call foreplay.

Coming to the mirror, Jean is suddenly and drunkenly maudlin.

JEAN

I'd never do that to Dave, even if I wanted. But it's just

like he's given up. Work, me, everything.

Sharon puts her arm around Jean's shoulders.

SHARON
Ah, love.

EXT. TOILETS. NIGHT

Thinking he recognises the distant and echoey voice, Dave stands up and tries to peer in the toilet window.

INT. TOILETS. NIGHT

Bee is standing in front of the urinals. She pulls her jeans half-way down her legs.

BEE
Here, love, this'll cheer you up. Wasn't in the Girl Guides for nowt . . .

Appalled, Gaz stares through the hole in the toilet door as Bee proceeds to piss standing up, straight into the urinal, just like a man. The other women stand back in uncontrollable giggles. To applause, Bee does herself up and the group crash back into the hall. A chastened Gaz creeps out of the urinal.

DAVE
(*off-screen; whispering*)
Gaz! Here, Gaz, was that our Jean?

GAZ
(*lying badly*)
Er, don't think so, Dave, no. Just some old tarts, like, you know. I'm going in for Nath.

INT. WORKING MEN'S CLUB. NIGHT

Gaz creeps into the hall full of women baying at an empty stage. A slow hand-clap has started. At the back, Nathan is pouring all the assorted drinks on one table into a pint glass.

He takes a quizzical look at it and downs it. Halfway through the drink, Gaz grabs him.

GAZ

You're in trouble, you. Come on.

NATHAN

What about Aunty Jean?

Gaz looks over at the group of women surrounding Jean. She is pummelling her arms like a steam train and roaring lecherously as the lights dim for the second half.

GAZ

Aunty Jean's busy.

EXT. SCHOOL. MORNING

Nathan and Gaz are walking side by side towards the school gates. Gaz is carrying Nathan's rucksack, Nathan is holding onto his sports bag and kicking it desultorily.

NATHAN

I don't feel well.

GAZ

'Course you don't, you cheeky chuffer, you've got a hangover. Listen, Nath, you don't have to go to school, you know. Take' day off, hang about at home.

NATHAN

Your house is messy.

GAZ

I'll clean it. We both could.

NATHAN

It's cold an' all.

GAZ

Alright, you could come down Job Club with us – it'll be a right laff.

NATHAN

Mum's house is allus warm.

GAZ

Yeah well. Can't always have the red carpet out, can I?
It's not her house anyway. It's what's-his-name's.
Barry's. Look, I'll do a big tidy around before next
weekend, alright? Promise. We could go see a footie
game?

NATHAN
(*brightening*)

Yeah?

GAZ

Yeah. They've got a Sunday League goin' down in the
park, now. Some good enough players.

*Nathan looks despondent again. They have reached the school
gates.*

NATHAN

United. Playing Man U on Saturday, aren't they?

GAZ

Nath . . . you know I can't stretch to that.

NATHAN

You're always making me do stupid stuff. Like last
night. Other dads don't do that.

GAZ

Don't they? Oh.

NATHAN
(*taking the rucksack*)

Bye.

*Nathan walks away, leaving Gaz lost for words. When he is
halfway down the path, Gaz shouts after him.*

GAZ

Nath, we can try an' sneak into Man U – Terry were telling us about this gap in' fence –

NATHAN
(*vehemently*)

– no!

DAVE
(*desperate*)

Alright, I'll get tickets, I will. 'Oo Ah, Cantona,' Nath, 'has to wear a girly bra . . .' We'll stuff 'em, eh Nath?

But Nathan has disappeared into the building. Gaz slams his forehead against the railings.

Fuck.

INT. JOB CLUB. MORNING

The walls of the Job Club are full of encouraging blue and yellow posters telling you how to apply for jobs. In the corner are boards with job vacancy cards. In the middle of the room, a group of hardened long-term unemployed, including Gaz and Dave, sit on DSS plastic bucket seats listening intently to the Job Club Manager who stands addressing them.

JOB CLUB MANAGER

I want your application letters finished by the time I get back, alright? Any problems, I'm outside.

As soon as the Job Club Manager leaves, ashtrays are brought out from hiding under the table, thermos flasks appear from nowhere and a pack of Top Trump cards materialises. The group of men shift their chairs to face Gaz. The men sort their hands while Gaz resumes his story.

GAZ

Me eyes have been opened, I can tell you. Standing up she were, straight into the what's-it, urinal jobby. Did you shuffle these, Terry, or what? When women start pissing like us, that's it, we're finished mate. Extincto.

Dave makes vague, ineffectual hand movements at his groin.

DAVE
But I mean . . . I mean, how . . . you know? How?

TERRY
(*darkly*)
Genetic mutation, intit? They're turning into us.

Gerald, an ex-foreman in his early forties who has ignored them up until now, swings angrily round from his computer screen.

GERALD
Button it, you lot, will you? Some of us are trying to get a job. Eh, and it says no smoking in 'ere.

GAZ
Yeah and it says Job Club up there and when were' last time you saw one of them walk in? You forget, you're not our foreman now, Gerald, you're just like the rest of us. Scrap.

GERALD
Just shut it, alright?

Gaz pulls a face at Gerald and turns back to his rapt audience.

GAZ
Mark me, give it a few years and men won't exist, 'cept in a zoo, or summat. I mean we're not needed no more, are we? What can lasses not do now, eh? Tell me one thing they can't do without us. One thing.

There is a silence as men inhale thoughtfully on their roll-ups.

Told you.

TERRY
(*triumphant*)
Babies. Worrabout babies? Let 'em try getting one in'
oven without us around. Now then . . .

GAZ
Babies be bollocksed. Nowadays it's a quick hand-
shandy in a test-tube and you're out the door, mate.

DAVE
Hey, you're not wrong neither.

GAZ
Obsolete, mate. Dinosaurs. Yesterday's news.

DAVE
(*after a morose pause*)
Like skateboards.

GAZ
Yeah. Like skateboards.

*Leaving his audience to mull over that, Gaz goes back to his
cards.*

DAVE
(*illuminated*)
Wait on, though. Why were them women all in' working
men's club in' first place, eh? Eh? Now then . . . 'cos of
us. Men.

GAZ
Call them Chippendales men? Degrading, that's worrit
was. Tell you, I've half a mind to become one of them
fuckin' feminist efforts.

Gaz picks up the Sun *and eyes up the Page 3 Girl without
enthusiasm.*

DAVE
How many lasses were there, though?

GAZ

Thousands. Baying for blood. Ten quid an' all! To watch some poof get his kit off. Ten quid . . .

DAVE

(*onto something*)

Right. Times ten quid by a thousand – and you've got . . .

(*gives up a brief attempt at counting*)

. . . yeah well, a lot. A very lot.

GAZ

(*thinking about it*)

Nah.

TERRY

Ten thousand quid!

GAZ

How much? Hey now, Dave, I mean, it's worth a thought, though, intit?

Turning from the computer, Gerald bursts into vicious laughter.

GERALD

Oh aye, can just see Little and Large prancin' around Sheffield with their widgers out – now that *would* be worth a tenner.

The laughter in the room begins to grow. Gaz backs down furiously.

GAZ

As if. Oh don't be so bloody daft. Were just saying, you know . . .

GERALD

Widgers on parade. Bring your own miroscope . . .

By now the laughter has turned into a roar. Gaz is eyeing up

Gerald blackly. It is only a matter of time. Oblivious, Gerald is wiggling his little fingers in unison. Dave unwisely chips in.

> DAVE
> I don't see why the chuff not, Gerald.

> GERALD
> Cos *you're* fat, and *you're* thin and you're *both* fuckin' ugly.

Uproar. Gaz dives across the table into Gerald's midriff. Amidst a flurry of fists and cheering they disappear under the table.

EXT. MANDY'S HOUSE. EVENING

Gaz walks up the path leading to a detached new house and knocks on the door. The door is opened by Mandy, a sharp-featured thirty-year-old: Gaz's ex-wife. Gaz thrusts a sheaf of papers at her.

> GAZ
> So what's all this sole custody bollocks?

> MANDY
> You know very well what it is. If you want joint custody, Garry, then you pay your share. Seven hundred quid I make it.

> GAZ
> I'm on the stripin' dole in case you haven't noticed.

> MANDY
> Then get a job – I'll *give* you a job –

> GAZ
> – two fifty an hour in the Black Hole of fucking Calcutta. No thank you.

> MANDY
> Fine. Whatever. If you want to go off and play your

games, you do that, Garry. But from now on Nathan's
going to have *two* parents.

GAZ

– right, yeah, and your bloody live-in lover's gonna do
that, is he? Oh abracadabra and 'ere he is. Evenin' Barry.

Barry, Mandy's partner has appeared at the doorway.

MANDY

That'll be for the Court to decide.

GAZ

No it won't. Nathan's yours and he's mine and he's fuck
all to do with him.

BARRY
(*shaking his head*)
As if you've ever given a toss.

MANDY

Face it, Garry, he doesn't even like staying at yours.

GAZ

'Course he bloody does. Ask him. Oi, Nath! We have a
laugh. Don't we, eh, kid?

*Gaz steps back from the doorway and looks up at the
bedroom windows.*

MANDY

Garry, don't.

GAZ

Is he in? Don't we Nath? Tell 'em.

But nobody comes to the window.

(*too offhand*)
Ah, he can't hear through your triple bloody glazing.

MANDY
(*gently*)
He can hear alright.

GAZ
It's wrong is this. It's all-to-fuckin'-cock. I'm his dad and
you – you're nobody.

BARRY
Goodnight, Garry.

Barry shuts the door on Gaz.

GAZ
Nobody!

Gaz steps back and looks up at the windows again.
(*forced cheerfulness*)
Night, Nathan. See you, eh?

EXT. MOORLAND ROAD. DAY

*On a deserted single-track road on the moors overlooking
Sheffield, two figures appear in running gear. Gaz and Dave
are labouring up the steep road. Gaz is dangling a pack of
cigarettes tantalisingly in front of Dave who is in real trouble,
wheezing badly. Dave makes an ineffectual grab for the
cigarettes.*

DAVE
No. Not doing it.

GAZ
Dave, they're taking him away. All I need is seven
hundred quid and they've got nowt on me.

DAVE
Gaz. No.

GAZ
Dave, he's me kid. Suppose there's nicking cars . . .

30

DAVE

No.

GAZ

Well then . . .

DAVE

I'll help, alright? I'm bloody running, aren't I? But I'm taking nowt off. Final.

They reach the crest of the hill. Dave is delighted to see a car parked up on a track off the road, its starter motor whirring ineffectually. At the wheel is Lomper, the security guard and cornet player.

GAZ
(*threatening*)

Dave, don't stop now, we're in trainin' . . .

Dave reaches the car and grinds to a halt.

DAVE

Good Samaritan – what can I do?

Watched by a perplexed Lomper, Dave rests on the bonnet in blissful relief.

GAZ

Oh aye? Well you know what else is passing by on t'other side – your bloody cigarettes.

DAVE

Gazza, yer tosser . . .

Gaz runs on. Recovering slightly, Dave motions the figure inside to pop the bonnet. Dave lifts it up and begins to delve expertly, coughing up half a lung all the while.

Just your H.T. leads, I reck.

Dave extracts the spark plug leads and gives them a polish on his T-shirt.

Yeah, you want new-uns, really. They're reet for a few
more miles yet, mind. Go on then.

*Lomper turns the keys and the car reluctantly starts. Pleased
with himself, Dave goes round to the driver's side window.
He is utterly oblivious to the hose-pipe that goes from the
exhaust into the car via the passenger window – not to
mention the fumes building up inside.*

DAVE
Hey, weren't you at Harrison's afore it closed?

Lomper nods dumbly as the car fills up with exhaust fumes.

(*pleased*)
Thought I clocked you. I were on 'floor' wi' Gaz – him
up' road. How's it going then? Got any work? Not a lot
about, is there?
(*getting no response*)
Aye, well, it's your connectors. Rub a bit of glass paper
on 'em when you get in, alright?

*Lomper nods blankly. With a shrug, Dave starts running
again.*

(*to himself*)
No, no, my chuffin' pleasure . . .

*Lomper lays his head back on the head-rest and closes his
eyes.*

EXT. MOORLAND ROAD. DAY

*Gaz has stopped on a bridge overlooking the motorway.
Slumped over the railings, he is deep into his cigarette when
he sees Dave coming. He lights another and holds it out like a
relay baton ready for Dave. Though exhausted, Dave is
looking unusually thoughtful as he trundles the last few yards.
He can't put his finger on it, but there's something wrong.
Approaching Gaz, Dave suddenly reacts as if electrocuted. He*

*screams, turns in his tracks and sprints as if possessed back
down the road.*

GAZ
(*waving the cigarette*)
Dave? Dave . . .!

EXT. MOORLAND ROAD. DAY

*Dave reaches Lomper's car and drags the choking figure out,
evidently just in time. Lomper lies on the ground, while Dave
paces up and down grasping his stomach and head, bellowing
in pain from his sprint, desperate for oxygen. He leans over
the prostrate Lomper.*

DAVE
Alright, kid?

Eventually, Lomper manages to speak.

LOMPER
Yer bastard.

*Still gasping, Dave raises his head, unable to believe his ears.
Then without a word, he picks up Lomper by the trousers,
hurls him back into the car and slams the door. Dave leans up
against the door drinking in the air wheezily, pointedly
ignoring the frantic knocking on the window. Far down the
road jogs a perplexed Gaz.*

GAZ
Dave . . .?

EXT. MOOR. DAY

*Gaz, Dave and Lomper lie in the heather gazing up into a
deep blue sky, smoking thoughtfully. After a long pause.*

DAVE
You could shoot yourself.

GAZ

Where's he gonna get a gun from round 'ere? Nah, you
wanna find a big bridge, you do.

DAVE

Yeah, like one of them bungee jumps. Just without the
bungee bit.

LOMPER

I can't stand heights, me.

DAVE
(*after some deep thinking*)
Drowning! Now then, there's a way to go . . .

LOMPER

Can't swim.

GAZ
(*getting impatient*)
You don't have to fuckin' swim, you divvy. That's the
whole point. God, you're not very keen are you?

LOMPER

Sorry.

Another long pause.

DAVE

I know. Stand in' middle of' road and get a mate to drive
smack into you really fast.

LOMPER

I don't have any mates.

Gaz rolls on top of Lomper and pulls his head up by the hair.

GAZ

Listen, you, we've just saved your fucking life, so don't
tell me I'm not your mate, alright?

34

LOMPER
(*a surprised smile*)

Yeah?

DAVE
(*hurt as well*)
Yeah. Me an' all. I'd run you down soon as look at you.

LOMPER
(*touched*)
Hey, ta lads. Ta very much.

INT. ROLLING MILL. NIGHT

Dave, Gaz and Nathan are waiting in the security guard's office where Lomper works. A bank of closed circuit TV monitors watch the building. Dave tries on Lomper's security guard hat.

DAVE
At least one bloke got a job out of this place being shut down, then. What you tell him for, anyroad? Kid's a nutter.

GAZ
He's a bugle player, isn't he? Right handy is that. We might need a bit of music. And he's got a car. Besides, good whatsaname for the lad. Therapy.

DAVE
Oh aye, jiggling about in the buff. Therapy. Tell you, he won't be' only one trying to top hisself if you carry on wi' this caper.

NATHAN
Dad, I'm hungry.

On one of the monitors, Lomper's car can be seen drawing up to the vast roller doors in the mill. Outside, a car horn honks twice.

INT. ROLLING MILLS OPERATION ROOM. NIGHT

*In the rolling mill operations room that oversees the whole
factory, Lomper wires an ancient record-player into the
Tannoy system. Down below on the factory floor Gaz,
Nathan and Dave are delving inside the bonnet of Lomper's
car. They bring out tin-foil cartons of Chinese food, almost
too hot to handle, from the heat of the engine. Crackle and
feed-back echo around the factory.*

                    DAVE
            (*surfacing from the engine*)
        Where's me rice then, Lomper?

                  LOMPER
            (*booming through the Tannoy*)
        Try the distributor, Four-eyes.

                    DAVE
        Watch it, you.

                  NATHAN
        I don't like Chinese.

                    GAZ
        You do. Don't you? Come on, it's hot, isn't it? Right.
        What records you brought, then, Lomper?

*Dave flicks through some of the records lying on the passenger
seat.*

                    DAVE
        Pink Floyd? Leonard Cohen? No wonder you're
        depressed. Ah, Rodney! Now you're talking – 'If Ya
        Think I'm Sexy, and You Want my Money . . .'

*Dave starts raunching around ridiculously to the tune, noodles
dripping from his mouth. Nathan looks on aghast.*

                    GAZ
        Stick it on then, Davereemo – I'm there.

*Gaz switches on the car headlights. Dave goes up to the
control room and kills the lights of the factory, leaving only a
dim glow in the operations room. He puts on the record as
Gaz stands in front of the car, silhouetted in the headlamp
beam, striking a dramatic pose. Nathan is dying quietly of
embarrassment.*

NATHAN

Dad . . . Dad don't.

GAZ
(without breaking his pose)
No, Nath, it's 'right. Seen 'em do it.

DAVE
(over the Tannoy)
Good evening shoppers. Today's special offer –

GAZ

Dave . . .!

DAVE
OK. Right. Sorry. Coming up. 'If You think I'm
Sexy . . .' A one, a two, a one two three four . . .

*Gaz turns from the crowd and crouches provocatively, head
hidden in his jean-jacket, waiting to explode with energy.
Instead, a crackly rendition of Rod Stewart's 'Sailing' moans
at them through the speakers. The atmosphere is ruined. Gaz
stands up, hands on hips, furious.*

GAZ

Oh for fuck's sake, Dave.

DAVE
(giggling, sheepish)
Sorry. Wrong side, wrong side. Sorry. OK right, got it.

*'If You Think I'm Sexy' begins to reverberate through the
rolling mill. Gaz starts strutting about and unbuttoning his*

jean-jacket. Lomper watches dispassionately, all the while sucking up long, stringy noodles into his mouth. Nathan squirms, barely able to watch. Gaz gets the jacket off and swings it raunchily around his head allowing his keys, cigarettes, lighter and a week's worth of change to scatter at high velocity in all directions. Lomper dives for cover behind a piece of machinery. Undaunted, Gaz begins to strip off his T-shirt. He gets it over his head where it sticks. There is a brief bit of wrestling inside the T-shirt before Dave takes the music off. Silence. Nathan takes his head out of his hands and creeps away.

GAZ
(*head still hidden in the T-shirt*)

I need an audience.

DAVE
(*over the Tannoy*)

You need a doctor.

INT. LOMPER'S CAR. NIGHT

Lomper is driving through empty, rain-swept Sheffield. Gaz is in the passenger seat, sulking. Dave is in the back. They are all staring out of the windows.

GAZ

You sure you checked the whole top-end?

LOMPER

Told you, he went out. I saw him go.

DAVE

There's the begger.

EXT. SHEFFIELD STREET. NIGHT

Gaz gets out of the car and catches up with Nathan who keeps walking.

38

GAZ

Nath. Nathan! Hell-fire, what you doing out here, kid?

NATHAN

Nowt. Walkin' home.

GAZ

It's miles home. You know that. Why'd you take off like that?

(no reply)

Eh? Nathan!

Gaz grabs Nathan and turns him around so they are facing each other.

You're embarrassed, aren't you? You think your own dad's a dick-head.

Nathan wrests himself free and marches on. Gaz follows.

I'm not doing this for a laff, you know. I'm trying to get some brass together so as you and me can keep seeing each other. They're trying to stop us, you see . . .

Nathan just keeps on walking. Gaz stops and watches him go.

May as well not bother. 'Cept that I'm your dad and that counts for summat, doesn't it? I – I like you. I love you, you bugger.

Nathan stops in his tracks. He turns round. Gaz walks up to him and crouches down beside him and cuffs him gently on the shoulder.

I could do with a hand, boss.

Nathan punches Gaz back. Gaz returns it a bit harder and Nathan really lets him have it on the shoulder. Gaz gathers him into a tight hug.

INT. LOMPER'S CAR. NIGHT

Gaz and Nathan get back in the car.

GAZ
Carry on, driver. Bit cold in here, Lomper.

Lomper switches on the heater. From nowhere, they are suddenly sprayed with rice.

DAVE
Eh, *there's* me fucking rice!

Gaz looks worriedly at Nathan: another cock-up. But for the first time, Nathan laughs.

INT. LOMPER'S HOUSE. NIGHT

At the bottom of a steep flight of stairs, an elderly, stern-looking woman hauls herself painfully out of a wheelchair. Leaning heavily on the banister, she begins an infinitely slow ascent of the stairs. After three or four steps, she hears the door slam but doesn't turn. Lomper arrives out of breath. His buoyancy is instantly deflated.

LOMPER
What you doing, Mum?

Without turning round, Lomper's Mum waves him away sharply.

LOMPER'S MUM
I can manage. Don't need *you* to get to me own bed.

LOMPER
I'm sorry. Lost track o' time.

Lomper's Mum takes another painful step.

LOMPER'S MUM
So where've you been?

LOMPER

Driving.

Lomper's Mum turns.

LOMPER'S MUM

Driving where?

LOMPER

Just driving.

LOMPER'S MUM

And what's the point of that?

LOMPER
(*shrugging hopelessly*)

There isn't any.

Silence. Each understands the other.

LOMPER'S MUM
(*softly*)

I thought you'd gone.

Lomper looks down at the floor and shakes his head slowly.

You going to leave me here all day?

Lomper walks up the stairs and gently lifts her into his arms.

INT. INFANTS' CLASS. NIGHT

*Standing on tiny wooden infants' chairs, Dave, Lomper,
Nathan and Gaz peer in between the children's 'stained-glass'
pictures of witches, ghouls and ghosties that cover the
windows of the school hall in preparation for Hallowe'en.
Through the glass they can see couples strutting around the
floor performing incredibly pompous, if technically perfect,
tangos. Nathan and Gaz get down from their chairs.*

NATHAN

Well you said dancin'.

41

GAZ

It were a great idea, kid, champion. It's just not the right
sort of dancing.

NATHAN
(*disappointed*)

Oh.

LOMPER

I don't believe it. It is . . .

DAVE

Gaz! Up 'ere!

*Gaz leaps back on his infant's chair. To his delight, he sees
Gerald and his manicured, uptight wife, Linda, sashaying
expertly around the dance floor.*

GAZ
(*evil delight*)

Oh my God. Look at the puffed-up chuffer – you just
wait, Gerald my lad, you're gonna be famous down' Job
Club.

DAVE

Hey, he's not bad for a bastard, though, is he?

GAZ

He's dead, that's what he is.

*As Gerald sashays smoothly past the windows, he spins himself
face to face with the four of them standing and pointing at
him like gargoyles. With a wickedly innocent smile, Gaz's
pointed hand turns into a slow and evil wave. Gerald's face
reveals the true horror of his predicament. Much too quickly
for Linda's liking, he dances her across to the other side of the
room. The four drop to the floor, giggling at their success.*

LOMPER

Well, you wanted a dance teacher.

DAVE

Gerald? Go get shagged – he'd tell every bugger – we'd
be laffed out of Sheffield.

*In the school hall, the music ends and Lomper stands up to see
what's going on. Gerald deposits Linda and makes his way
over to them.*

LOMPER

Eh up, lads, bandits at six o'clock.

INT. INFANTS' CLASS ROOM. EVENING

*Gerald enters the classroom to be confronted by the three
lounging over-casually on the tiny infant chairs smoking roll-
ups. Among the infant school paraphernalia, Gaz is vaguely
messing about in the sand-tray and Dave has discovered some
plastic throwing rings. He slips them onto his wrist absent-
mindedly.*

GAZ

Torvil, come in, come dancing, come where you like –
park your sequins over here.

GERALD

Alright alright. You've had your little laff, now piss off.

LOMPER

Free country.

GAZ

I thought you were rather good, actually. Very nifty
footwork.

From down the corridors comes Linda's voice.

LINDA
(*off-screen*)

Gerald? Gerald?

Linda appears at the door.

Oh. Hello. Gerald, we're missing the rumba.

GERALD
Sorry love, just been talking to some mates from, er,
work.

*Gaz and Lomper exchange puzzled glances. Gerald looks
pleadingly at them. Dave is more worried about the plastic
rings that have jammed firmly on his wrist.*

LINDA
(*worried*)
Oh. Not thinking of joining our class?

GAZ
Well, funny you should mention it –

GERALD
(*hustling her out*)
– we should be getting back, Linda.

LINDA
Well goodnight.

GAZ
You get back to your rumba. We'll be seeing you later,
then, Gerald. At er, work, eh?

Gerald and Linda exit.

EXT. GERALD'S STREET. MORNING

*Hunched against the cold, Gaz and Dave are lurking around
the gate to Gerald's house. Impatient, Dave peers into the
garden. Gaz is coughing violently on his first roll-up of the
day.*

GAZ
(*in between coughs*)
Die, yer bastard.

                    DAVE
                  (*darkly*)
He's got gnomes.

                    DAVE
Aye, he bloody would have.
                  (*tutting*)
You're gonna be late for Job Club, Gerald.

INT. GERALD'S HOUSE. MORNING

*Wearing her dressing-gown, Linda is as usual preparing a
packed lunch in the kitchen for Gerald. Unusually cheerful,
Gerald is humming to himself as he does up his tie in the
mirror.*

                    LINDA
Things looking up?

                    GERALD
D'you know, I think they just might be, yeah.

                    LINDA
Good. You've been working too hard. It's about time
one of your colleagues did the lion's share for a change. I
wish you'd be firmer, Gerald.

*Uncomfortable with the conversation, Gerald moves away
from the mirror and picks up his briefcase.*

                    GERALD
Mustn't be late.

                    LINDA
So it's alright if I . . .?

Linda waves some skiing brochures at him.

                    GERALD
Linda – I don't know.

LINDA

Oh don't be so mean. Things are looking up, you said so yourself. You'll love skiing.

GERALD

Linda I –

Gerald looks at Linda for a second as if he might tell her everything, then heads for the door.

Bye.

EXT. GERALD'S STREET. MORNING

Gerald walks down his path and bumps straight into Gaz and Dave, who has formed an acquaintance with one of the gnomes.

GAZ

Off to the 'office', are we, Torvil?

GERALD

As a matter of fact, yes. I bloody am.
                    (*to Dave and his gnome*)
Put that back.

Gerald marches down the street, with Gaz and Dave in pursuit. Gerald delves inside his briefcase and brings out a letter which he waves.

See this? Interview. In the bloody bag, mate – I know him from Harrisons – could do the job standing on me head. And I won't have to see your ugly mugs ever again.

GAZ

We just need your help a bit.

GERALD
                    (*utterly dismissive*)
Sorry pal, there's nothing I could do to help the likes of you. Nothing.

Just wanted to know about dancin', that's all.

Gerald laughs derisively.

GERALD
Dancers have co-ordination, skill, timing, fitness and grace. Take a long hard look in the mirror. Now I'm busy. Don't be late for' Job Club, lads.

Gerald marches off, leaving them standing. From nowhere, the Roller-blader shoots through the tiny gap between Gaz and Dave and streaks off into the distance.

GAZ
Oi, Starlight Express, I'll have you . . .

INT. INTERVIEW ROOM. DAY

Gerald sits in front of a board of company Directors. He looks quite confident about the whole affair.

GERALD
. . . it's not been an easy six months, granted, but I've kept myself . . .

Gerald's voice tails away. At the window behind the Directors, Gerald could have sworn he saw a gnome on a rope swing from one side of the window to the other.

. . . busy, yes.

DIRECTOR
Well all the qualifications are there, obviously, Gerald, and we go back further than I care to remember –

But the Director can see that Gerald's attention is no longer with him. He is staring over the Director's shoulder at a gnome that is trolling along the bottom of the window. Gerald tries to recover.

Sorry?

Puzzled, the Director turns just as the gnome disappears from view. All he sees is an empty window.

DIRECTOR
(getting impatient)
What we're asking, Gerald, is, after such a long lay-off, d'you think you're up to the job?

The gnome has appeared on the window ledge again, this time being pursued by another gnome. A silent 'argument' takes place between the two before one gnome nuts the other. The plaster head falls off. Gerald looks utterly lost. The Directors look meaningfully at each other and, as one, turn to their notes.

INT. JOB CLUB. DAY

The Job Clubbers are sitting in twos either side of plastic tables. Mock interviews. The Job Club Manager patrols behind the interviewees listening to their answers.

TERRY
Well I've got me class two HGV licence, and I've done a lot of driving in me time.

JOB CLUB MANAGER
That's good. Positive answers.

The Job Club Manager moves on to the next table where Gaz is being interviewed by Dave. Totally in character, Dave waves the CV in his hand, tuts and shakes his head sadly.

DAVE
I'm terribly sorry, Mr Schofield, I don't think a City and Guilds in Catering really qualifies you to be a helicopter pilot.

GAZ

I know *everything* about helicopters. And you're
forgetting my CSE in metal-work, Mr Horsfall.

DAVE
(*quick as a flash*)
What's the top speed of a Chinook, then?

GAZ
(*even quicker*)
Four hundred and twenty miles an hour.

DAVE
(*rolling the 'r'*)
Wro . . . ng!

*Suddenly the door to the Job Club crashes open. Gerald
stands there, shaking with rage.*

GERALD
(*pointing*)
You . . . You bastard.

*Gerald charges towards Gaz. The Job Clubbers scatter as Gaz
leaps to his feet and gets a table between him and Gerald.*

GAZ
Hey, Gerald, mate, now Gerald . . .

GERALD
Come here, you, I'm gonna kill you.

GAZ
Now Gerry . . .

Gerald chases Gaz around the table.

GERALD
Gonna kill you.

GAZ
You didn't get it, then?

Gerald roars and throws the table against the wall. Gaz breaks for the door and makes it as far as the corridor before Gerald grabs him.

INT. JOB CENTRE CORRIDOR. DAY

Gerald forces Gaz up against the wall as the rest of the Job Clubbers peer through the door at the action. Dave intervenes, trying to restrain Gerald.

> DAVE
> Come on now, youth, calm down.

> GERALD
> Bastard, bastard. Get off.

> GAZ
> Leave him, Dave.

> DAVE
> Eh?

> GAZ
> I said leave him, alright? Go on, then Gerald, do your worst. I'd fucking hit *you*, mate, so go on, lam in.

Gerald loosens his hold on Gaz. In place of the aggression, there is desperation bordering on panic.

> GERALD
> Bastard. That were mine. You don't know what it's like, you – you . . . jokers. You don't give a toss. You're kids. It's different for me. I've got a standard of living. Responsibilities. I were on me way up. I am on me way up.

Gerald slumps down on the crash mat.

> First interview in months. They knew me. I could have got me first month in advance and she'd never have known. Now what?

He looks up at Gaz and Dave. They say nothing.

> She's still got the credit cards, y'know. She's out there
> now, loose on the high street with a Barclaycard,
> *spending.*
>> (*despair*)
> You bastard. Why d'you do that? That were mine that
> job. It were mine. It had to be.

*Gaz and Dave stare at a broken man. Nobody knows what to
say.*

GAZ
Could you not . . . I dunno – tell her?

GERALD
Tell her? After six months? How can I tell her? A
woman who wants to go skiing for us holidays? Skiing
for Christ's sake!

*Shaking his head, Gerald gets to his feet and walks slowly out.
The three of them stand awkwardly, ashamed.*

DAVE
I've only ever been sledging, me.

EXT. SHEFFIELD PARK. DAY

*Surrounded by graffiti and rubbish, Gerald shelters forlornly
in the vandalised bandstand. A flock of pigeons peck around
him hopefully. Gerald delves inside his briefcase and pulls out
his lunch-box and the application letter. He tears it into small
bits and feeds it to the pigeons. Absently he opens his lunch-
box only to find it stuffed with sticks of celery and carrot. He
bites a chunk of celery and chews dismally before spitting it
out and feeding the rest to the pigeons. Gaz, Nathan, Lomper
and Dave wander into view. They approach Gerald
sheepishly.*

GERALD

Can't you just leave me alone?

Dave steps forward very seriously, holding the gnomes.

DAVE

Super-glued it. Can hardly see the join, look.

Gerald searches their faces, looking for the malicious joke.
Cautiously, Gerald takes the gnomes and scrutinises Dave's
handiwork. Then Gaz holds out a tiny wooden wheelbarrow
to Gerald.

GAZ

Got it in' jumble, like. To say sorry.

DAVE

Wheel goes round and everything.

LOMPER

It's for your gnomes really, not you, but . . .

Gerald takes the wheelbarrow. He examines it, overcome
with emotion. Gaz, Lomper, Nathan and Dave stand
awkwardly.

GERALD

I, er, I – I don't know – it's, er, marvellous is this,
fucking marvellous.

GAZ

We were thinking you could put it next to' wishing well.
Make a bit of a whatsaname – *feature* of it, like. What
d'you reck?

Gerald turns his back to them, fighting to keep his emotions
under control.

GERALD

Ta, lads, eh? Ta very much.

Gerald keeps his back to them. Gaz stares resolutely into the

middle distance, himself close to tears. He holds out two
fingers to Dave.

> GAZ
>
> Cigarette me, for fuck's sake.

EXT. PARK. DAY

Dave, Lomper, Nathan, Gaz and Gerald walk through the
park. As if watching the ducks, they stop to watch a group of
teenagers spinning the round-a-bout in the children's play
area. An eight-year-old younger brother is being spun on it
mercilessly fast.

> GAZ
>
> Think any of that could dance?

> LOMPER
>
> Load of piss artists.

> GERALD
>
> You're not still on for this Chippendales malarkey, are
> you?

> GAZ
>
> Yorkshire version, like. Them buggers do it, so we
> bloody could.

The youngster on the round-a-bout finally succumbs to
centrifugal force and flies off into the mud where he remains
motionless. The show over, the gang turn, impassive, and
continue to walk.

> GERALD
>
> But you can't dance.

> GAZ
> *(pointedly)*
>
> We know, Gerald.

A Woman in her early twenties totters towards them in a tight
leather mini-skirt and high heels. Dave sees her coming.

DAVE
Eh up, Gaz. Niner on its way.

Gaz glances up briefly, amazingly registers no interest at all and goes back to his discussion with Gerald.

GAZ
Why d'you think we're trailing you all over town?

GERALD
(*mulling*)
Oh I don't know. It's not my kind of dancing, is it? It's all arse-wiggling and that.

GAZ
Listen, I've got a City and Guilds in arse-wiggling, mate. You learn us dancing and I'll learn you' rest. Gerald, for once I'm dead serious. I need your help.

GERALD
What if someone spots me? What if Linda finds out? I've got standing, I 'ave.

GAZ

Aye, and you've an overdraft an' all, matey.

INT. BURGER BAR. DAY

The gang are enviously watching Nathan devour a burger and a plateful of chips. A good-looking painter/decorator type in his mid-twenties walks past towards the till. Just as Gaz usually does with women, he swings round to stare at the man.

GAZ

A six? Seven out of ten if he sorted that pig-tail out. He'd do nicely for us. There's talent everywhere, Gerry mate.

GERALD

Forced to admit, nice pair of legs.

Absently, Gerald dips into Nathan's chips.

DAVE
(*worried*)

Summat's up wi' you lot.

GAZ
(*dipping into the chips*)

Dave, get us another Coke for' lad, there's a mate.

Dave gets up, then pauses, waiting for the money.

(*hissing*)

Told you, I'll pay you back.

(*pleading*)

Dave . . .

Dave takes a handful of chips and trundles off, muttering.

(*to Nathan*)

This is proper, eh, Nath? Quarter-pounder an' all. Real proper.

Nathan nods happily. Over at the counter, a television is showing a 100 metres sprint. In slow motion, a black athlete breaks the tape. Mouth full of chips, Gaz nods towards it.

That's what we're after.

LOMPER

A sprinter?

GAZ

No, a blackie. Every lass's fantasy, is that. You just watch and tell me the rumours aren't true.

LOMPER

That's bollocks, that is.

The TV reruns the race in glorious close up. The athlete's indubitably impressive lunch-box fills the screen. Dave grimaces and comes back to the table with the Coke.

DAVE
(*picks up another chip*)
Shouldn't be allowed on telly, that.

NATHAN

Oi!

GAZ

That, gentlemen, is a lunch-box to be proud of.

LOMPER

Don't look right comfy, mind.

DAVE

Neither would yours at thirty mile an hour.

GAZ
(*dreaming*)
Think of that on stage, lads. Lights . . . music . . . lunch-box. Hell-fire, they'd be eating chips out of our knickers.

Gaz takes a thoughtful chip. Nathan finally cracks.

                    NATHAN
  Will you get off my chips!

The gang are silenced – and a bit hurt – by this unexpected outburst.

                    GERALD
  Well let's find one, then.

                    GAZ
  One what?

Gerald nods towards the pictures of the athlete.

                  (*over-casual*)
  You, er . . . in then?

                    GERALD
                  (*shrugging*)
  Chuff-all else to do.

                    GAZ
  Nice one, Gerald.

INT. DAVE'S HOUSE. NIGHT

Jean is in bed reading a magazine. Dave is in the bathroom getting undressed. He takes off his shirt and stares unhappily in the mirror, gripping onto the fleshy tyre around his waist with both hands.

                    DAVE
  I say Jean?

                    JEAN
                  (*off-screen*)
  Yeah?

                    DAVE
  Have you ever, er . . . ever been out with a black bloke, like?

Dave pulls his trousers off and stands in his boxer shorts on the weighing scales, rocking on them in order to get the lowest possible reading. When this doesn't work, he stands on one leg, wobbling furiously during the conversation.

>   JEAN
>   (*off-screen*)
> You know I haven't, Dave.

>   DAVE
> They're crap, these. I'm the same as last week. But if you were on the look-out for another fella, right . . . if you were, like, just saying, would you think about it?

>   JEAN
>   (*off-screen*)
> What's got into you?

Dave gets off the scales and stands in the bedroom doorway.

>   DAVE
> No, would you though?

Jean takes him seriously this time.

>   JEAN
>   (*seriously*)
> I might do, Dave, yeah. That alright?

>   DAVE
> So it's true then.

Dave goes back to the bathroom and puts on his pyjamas.

>   JEAN
>   (*off-screen*)
> I've had enough of this. What's bloody true?

>   DAVE
> About black men. You know, that they've got great bodies an' – an' that.

> JEAN
> (*off-screen*)

Some of them, yeah.

Staring in the mirror, Dave squeezes his droopy breasts painfully.

And?

> DAVE

Nothing.

Troubled, Dave goes through to the bedroom and gets into bed.

> JEAN

David, what is this all about? I don't care whether they're black, white or bloody rainbow flavour. I'm married to *you*. Remember?

> DAVE

Yeah. Night.

Dave switches off the bedside light. Jean settles down in bed facing Dave's huge back. She traces a finger across his shoulders.

> JEAN

Why would I want anyone else, eh, Big Man?

Her finger begins to run down Dave's side. Without turning, Dave puts a restraining hand on top of hers. He pats it weakly.

> DAVE

I'm all in, Jeanie.
> (*attempt at a joke*)
It's amazing how tiring it is doing nowt, y'know.

Pained, Jean withdraws her hand and turns away from Dave.

> JEAN

There are jobs going at Woolies, if you want 'em.

Security guard's going – or shelf stackers. Even go on'
tills.

                          DAVE
Women's work.

                          JEAN
Well, whatever makes you happy, Dave.

*Jean stares miscrably out of the bed. Dave lies on the other
side of the bed, biting his lip.*

INT. BRASS BAND HUT. DAY

*Lanky, hyperactive and jittery, Ross, a lad in his early
twenties, paces around ceaselessly in front of the Gang, pulling
nervously at his greasy hair. The Gang are sitting behind a
trestle table, as if interviewing candidates. Gerald is hiding
behind a paper and all that can be seen of Dave is a pair of
legs sticking out from behind a filing cabinet.*

                          GAZ
Er, right then, if you'd like to hand your tape to yer man
there, he'll stick it on and er, away you go.

                          ROSS
How much?

                          GAZ
Eh?

                          ROSS
How much? How much you offering? Eh?

                          LOMPER
It's an audition, mate.

                          ROSS
Do it for twenty, like. Eh? What d'you say, eh? Blow job
for a tenner, eh? What d'you say?

Dave emerges from behind the filing cabinet.

DAVE

Go home, Ross. There's a good lad.

ROSS

Oh alright, Dave? Eh? Not so bad, eh? Good mate is
Dave. What about it then, eh?

DAVE
(*quietly*)

Ross, I said go home.

*Ross looks at Dave blankly then drops his head and shuffles
out. At the doorway, he turns.*

ROSS

Give you a hand-job for a fiver, eh?

DAVE
(*as if to a bad dog*)

Home!

Ross disappears.

Lives down our road. His dad knocks him about.

GERALD

This is crazy.

CUT TO:

*The Horse, a frail black man in his late forties who stands
awkwardly in front of the panel. They aren't impressed.*

GAZ

So, er, it's Mr Horse, is it?

HORSE

Just Horse.

GAZ

Right, yeah, OK. Er, just a minute, Horse, my colleagues
on the panel . . .

LOMPER
(*whispering*)
Ask him *why's* he's called The Horse.

GAZ
(*whispering*)
You bloody ask him. It's not 'cos he does the Grand
National, is it?

GERALD
(*whispering*)
That's all very well, but what use a big wanger if you
need a bloody zimmer frame to tout it about, eh? He
must be fifty if he's a day.

GAZ
So Horse, what er can you do?

HORSE
Well, I – dunno really . . . let's see. The Bump, the
Stomp, the Bus Stop – my break-dancin' days are
probably over – but there's always the Funky Chicken –

GERALD
(*impressed*)
Now you're talking, mate.

GAZ
What, all of them?

HORSE
Yeah, I think so. It's been a while, mind. And I've a
dodgy hip right now . . .

GAZ
Yeah? Well, stick it on, Nath. Do your worst, pal.

*Nathan cues up the tape. A funky number fills the room. The
Horse begins to move, painfully slowly at first, old limbs
remembering the sequences. The Gang exchange disappointed*

looks. Then gradually the music flows through his bones until he is grooving sinuously around the floor, spinning, twisting and funking that chicken – much to Dave's delight. The song comes to an impressive end with a whoop and an attempted, though only partially successful, splits. To applause from Dave and Nathan, the Horse painfully gets to his feet.

HORSE

Like I said. Me hip.

GAZ

Sod the hip, mate. You're in.

CUT TO:

Reg, a man in his late forties, carrying two heavy bags of shopping into the band hut.

REG
(*shrugging*)

Shall I start then?

Nathan puts on the tape and Reg begins taking his clothes off with less and less enthusiasm to the infinitely unerotic strains of stripping music. He gets his trousers halfway down before coming to a halt. Sadly, he shakes his head and pulls them up again. Nathan switches off the music.

Sorry, I . . . Sorry. Thought I'd give it go. Got a bit desperate, like. You know how it is. Can't even take me kit off properly though, can I?

Aware that Reg is close to the edge, Gaz stands up.

GAZ

You're alright, Reg, no problem. Got a cuppa tea here if you're interested.

REG

No ta. Got the kids outside.

                              GAZ
    Bring 'em in.

                              REG
    Nah, this is no place for kids.

Gaz looks across at Nathan as Reg gathers up his clothes from
the floor and walks out. Gaz sits down heavily.

CUT TO:

Guy, a gentle hunk of a plasterer in his mid-twenties who is
sitting eagerly in front of the panel. Gerald whispers to Gaz.

                              GUY
    I've always wanted to be a dancer. Me favourite film's
    Singin' in' Rain. They do that walking up' wall thing.
    Bloody ace, it is.

                            GERALD
    I've seen him before. He plastered our bathroom a while
    back. He knows me. Get rid of him, he'll blow me cover.

                              GAZ
    Keep your trap shut, you'll be fine. What walking up
    wall thing?

                              GUY
    Show you. I'm Donald O'Connor, right?

The panel watch as Guy stands up and runs towards the wall.
Somehow he manages to get both legs up the wall so that for a
split second he is suspended horizontal to the floor. The next
second he crashes flat onto the floor. He lets out the wheeze of
the terminally wounded.

                              GAZ
                       (*trying to be kind*)
    Great.

GUY
(*getting up, winded*)
It's better than that in the film.

GERALD
So. You don't sing.

GUY
No.

GAZ
You don't dance.

GUY
No.

GAZ
Hope you don't think I'm nosy, but what the chuff *do* you do?

GUY
(*uncertain*)
Well . . . there is this.

Guy pulls the belt out of his trousers and pulls them down in one movement. The faces on the Gang – a mixture of awe, shock and respect – betray Guy's unique talents.

GAZ
Gentlemen, the lunch-box has landed.

Forgetting himself, Gerald lowers the protective Daily Mirror *for the first time that day.*

GERALD
Chuffin' Nora.

GUY
(*instantly recognising the voice*)
Oh hello, Gerald, I didn't recognise you there. I did his bathroom.

Gerald tries to hide behind his paper again, then gives up.

GERALD
(grumpy)
Hello, Guy.

Gaz suddenly remembers Nathan and waves frantically at him to stop looking. But Nathan is transfixed.

GAZ
Nathan! Nathan . . .!

INT. WOOLWORTHS. DAY

Half-hidden by a rail of nighties, Dave is watching Jean working in the bathroom accessories aisle. She is admiring a male sales assistant, Franko, who is juggling expertly with three nailbrushes for her benefit. Though Dave is too far away to hear, he can see them giggling conspiratorially. Dave looks deeply worried. Gaz appears at his shoulder, also staring at Jean and Franko.

GAZ
They're just messing, Davo.

DAVE
You think?

GAZ
'Course. Just Jean, innit?

Dave trundles back to the gang, followed by Gaz. The rest of the Gang are hanging around the video section of the store, pulling change out of their pockets and counting up. Dave sidles up to Nathan who is delving in a bag of pick 'n' mix.

DAVE
Got any of them mint and chocolate jobs, Nath?

NATHAN
Get lost. You're on a diet.

DAVE

Don't you start an' all.

GAZ

Oi, Dave, how much you got then?

DAVE
(*digging around*)
Twenty-two, twenty-seven pence.

GAZ

'Kin great. We're about a fiver short, then. You know
what that means, Dave.

DAVE

Oh no, Gaz, come on . . . why me?

GAZ
(*chucking Dave under the chin*)
'Cos you've got an innocent face, love. I've got serial
killer written on me forehead. And if you're not gonna
dance you can bloody well do summat useful.

DAVE

Jean'll throw an eppy if she finds out. She's only o'er
there.

GAZ

She's miles away. Right, we'll be waiting outside with the
pick 'n' mix, won't we, Nath?
(*saluting*)
Good luck, corporal.

DAVE
(*to Nathan*)
Give us a pear drop, you.

NATHAN

They're not paid for . . .

Dave snatches a pear drop from Nathan's bag of sweets and

67

the Gang disperse innocently. He picks out the video he is looking for and as he bends down to retie a shoe lace, drops the video into the open top of his jacket.. As he straightens up he looks nervously around and permits himself a small smile as he realises that he has got away with it. As reward, he pops the pear drop into his mouth, whereupon every alarm in the world goes off. Dave panics. Convinced, in his dietary guilt, that he has eaten an alarm-activated pear drop, he spits it out onto his hand and stares at it. The alarms continue to ring. He drops the sweet onto the floor and stamps on it, hoping to stop the alarms that way. Miraculously, the store falls silent. Dave shakes his head in wonderment at such high-tech confectionery and walks out of the doors. Every alarm in the building goes off.

INT. ROLLING MILL. NIGHT

Inside the night-watchman's office the only light comes from the bank of closed-circuit televisions that display various areas of the deserted factory. The Gang are sitting around happily eating pick 'n' mix, except for Dave who is in the blackest of moods.

Gerald puts a tape in – Flashdance. *A welding scene comes up.*

> DAVE
> *(after a few seconds)*
> Eh? What's *she* bloody doing? I didn't go on the nick in
> Woolies for a women's bloody DIY video . . .

> GAZ
> *Flashdance*, Dave. She's a welder, isn't she? Don't you
> know nowt?

> DAVE
> *(scornfully)*
> Welder . . . well I hope she can dance better than she
> welds – look at the state o' that. Her mix is all to cock.

GAZ

Shut up, will you, Divvo. What the fuck do you know
about welding, anyroad?

Dave marches up to the video and presses pause.

DAVE

More than a chuffing woman. 'S like bloody bonfire
night – too much acetylin is that. Them joints won't
hold fuck-all.

GERALD
(*pressing play again*)
For Christ's sake, Dave, we're watching for the dancing,
aren't we?

GAZ

He's just got the hump on about Woolies.

Forgotten in the row, Lomper is studying the video intently.

LOMPER

Oi! Cop a load of this.

He presses a button on the desk and Flashdance *explodes onto
all the monitors on the wall. Gaz and Dave are stopped in
their tracks by the woman's superb dancing.*

GAZ
(*impressed*)

Strap back.

GERALD

Told you, didn't I? Nifty on her pins is that 'un. That,
gentlemen, is what we're after.

DAVE

As if.
(*points at Gaz*)
How's *he* ever gonna do all that twizzling-about
bollocks?

GERALD

Just a souped-up tango is that. Teach any bugger in a week. Even you, mate.

DAVE

A fat bastard like me? I know what I am, Gerald, so don't take the piss.

GERALD

Alright, two weeks. Straight up.

EXT. STREET BY STEELWORKS. NIGHT

Dave and Gaz trudge down the street.

DAVE

Jean reckons I should take that security guard job down at Woolies.

GAZ

Well it'll make a change to nicking from there. Security. You're worth more than that, Davo.

DAVE

Jean don't think so. I reckon there's summat going on wi' her and that bloke.

GAZ
(*unconvincing*)
The juggling bugger? Nah. No way.

DAVE
(*almost to himself*)
It's not as if I'd blame her.

GAZ

You could show her, Dave. Nobody tells them Chippendale efforts to go be security, do they? Raking it in they are.

(*pause*)

Two weeks he said, Dave. He's not taking the piss, honest.

DAVE

It's a thought.

GAZ

It's more than a thought. Any old hippy can juggle. But think of Jean's face when she sees you – dancin' like old fuckin' *Flashdance*, eh?

A smile of enlightenment comes to Dave's face.

DAVE

Two week? Just like old flashy tits?

GAZ

'S what your man said.

DAVE

Hey, I can weld better than her, an' all.

INT. ROLLING MILL. DAY

With their arms clamped firmly to their sides, Guy, the Horse, Gaz and Dave are standing in a staggered row like so many toy soldiers. Nathan switches on a cassette player and the music starts.

GERALD

Forward!

Dave and Lomper move one step forward, making the row even more staggered. Gerald is nearing the end of his patience.

No, no, no. You –
(*manhandling Lomper back a step*)
– stay put. And you –

71

> (*manhandling Gaz*)
> – go forward. Let's try again . . . Nathan!
> (*Nathan rewinds the music*)
Forward!

Lomper moves forward again with a purposeful stride, sees Gerald's face and moves swiftly back two paces. The line is once again a shambles.

Stop!

LOMPER

Sorry.

GERALD

Jesus Christ, Einstein, all I want is to get you in a straight bloody line. What do I have to do?

The Gang look at their feet, crestfallen.

HORSE

Well it's the Arsenal off-side trap, isn't it?

GERALD

You what?

HORSE

Arsenal off-side trap. Lomper's Tony Adams, right? When any bugger looks like scoring, you step forward in a line and wave your arms about like a fairy.

DAVE
(*enlightened*)

Ohh. Well that's easy.

Nathan starts the music again.

GERALD

Forward!

The Gang move from their staggered position into a perfect straight line. Gerald fails to hide his annoyance.

Perfect. Perfect.

> DAVE
> Well you should have said.

EXT. GERALD'S HOUSE. DAY

The Gang are on the doorstep of Gerald's house. He opens the door and ushers them in.

> GERALD
> Come on, get in quick. And wipe your boots.

Gerald hurries them in, looking nervously about him before shutting the door.

INT. GERALD'S HOUSE. DAY

The Gang look uncomfortable in Gerald's rather prim living room. Lomper settles on the settee with a copy of Country Life *while Dave fiddles with some nasty glass ornaments on the mantelpiece.*

> GERALD
> Put them down, you'll break 'em.

> DAVE
> Just looking. Right posh, isn't it?

> LOMPER
> Get a brew on, eh?

> GAZ
> Haven't time for that. Right then, are we right?

> HORSE
> Right for what?

> GAZ
> Taking us kit off.

                    LOMPER
                   (*astounded*)
You what?

                    DAVE
                   (*aggrieved*)
Thought you were turning me into a fancy dancer.

                    GAZ
Listen, ladies, we're strippers, aren't we?

                    GERALD
What, right now? Here? In my house? This is a good
area round here, you know.

Gerald runs over to the window and closes the curtains.

                    DAVE
Gaz, I don't know . . .

                    GAZ
If we can't get us kit off in front of us selves, how the
hell are we going to in front of all them lasses? C'mon.
Tops off.

                    DAVE
No looking – and no laffing, you bastards.

*Keeping their eyes very much to themselves, everyone begins
to take off their shirts.*

                    LOMPER
What are we doing? What are we doing?

                    GERALD
I used to have a real job, me.

                    GAZ
And your kegs.

*Eventually the team are standing in various states of
underpant. Everyone stares at everyone else, shyly at first,*

74

then plucking up courage they begin to look at each other's bodies. The Horse is wearing the most bizarre underclothes – thermal plus fours that bag hugely between his legs. Gaz and Gerald exchange glances.

GAZ

Horse by name, horse by nature, eh, Horse?

HORSE
(*deeply uncomfortable*)

Shut it, you.

GUY
(*to Gerald*)

How come you're so brown, anyroad?

GERALD

No reason.

GUY

Someone's got a sunbed, haven't they, Gerald?

Whistles and coy noises from the Gang.

GERALD

It's Linda's and no you bloody can't, so don't even think about asking.

Dave stares down at his stomach sorrowfully.

DAVE

So what am I supposed to do wi' this?

Gaz prodes the bulk experimentally with a finger, eyes it in profile.

GAZ
(*unconvincingly*)

Well, I mean it's not too bad . . . from the front, like.

GERALD
(*with gravitas*)
Fat, David, is a feminist issue.

DAVE
And what's that supposed to mean when it's at home?

GERALD
I don't bloody know, do I? It just is, alright?

DAVE
I try dieting – I do try. Feels like I've been on a fuckin'
diet all me life. The less I eat, the fatter I bloody get. It's
not meant to work like that, is it?

LOMPER
So stuff yourself and get thin.

DAVE
Oh shut up, saggy-tits.

LOMPER
I have not . . .

GERALD
Mate of Linda's had this plastic stuff put on her down at
some posh clinic – took off stones it did, like magic –
what were it called, now? Just like cling-film it were –

DAVE
(*outraged*)
– cling-film? I'm not a chicken drumstick, Gerald.

*Suddenly there is a knock at the door. The team are paralysed
with fear. Gerald is the first to panic. He throws himself into
his clothes.*

GERALD
'Kin hellfire. Get in the kitchen, go on.

LOMPER
(*ever hopeful*)
Can we have a brew?

GERALD
No!

INT. KITCHEN. DAY

Still only in their underpants, the Gang hide in the kitchen.
Lomper is going through the cupboards, examining different
boxes of herbal tea suspiciously.

LOMPER
(*whispering*)
Dandelion? Rosehips? Weeds. In us fuckin' tea . . .

INT. LIVING ROOM. DAY

Two large men push into the room, followed by a furious
Gerald.

GERALD
You can't just take stuff.

MAN 1
Sorry, mate.

The other Man proceeds to unplug the television and video.

GERALD
I only owe him a hundred and twenty quid.

MAN 1
Aye that's all these'll fetch second-hand.

GERALD
They're not second-hand.

MAN 2
(*picking up the television*)
They are now, mate.

Suddenly, Dave's monstrous near-naked body appears in the door. He has a tea-towel wrapped around his mouth, disguising his identity.

DAVE

Alright, boys?

The rest of the Gang follow Dave into the room.

MAN I

'kin hell . . .

DAVE

Put down and piss off.

Dave puts both hands around his belly and takes a step towards them. Confronted with five strange men in their underpants, the two men flee without another word.

GERALD
(*morose*)

Cheers, lads.

DAVE

Hey, it's alright is this stripping lark.

EXT. ROLLING MILL. DAY

Sheffield's dilapidated warehouses and mills stretch into the distance – a depressing sight were it not for the faint but funky music pulsing from the rolling mill.

INT. ROLLING MILL. DAY

The Gang are on the factory floor in a clearing surrounded by machine tools. Music is reverberating around the mill. Perched on a machine, Nathan watches the Gang, led by Gerald, go tentatively through the beginnings of a dance routine that does indeed resemble a football line-up.

GERALD
(*over the music*)
Up the wings, Gaz and Lomps, two three four and left
touch-line two three right touch-line two three and off-
side trap . . . now. Then the belt, two three four . . .

*With one flourish, Gerald whips the belt out of his trousers,
slapping Guy smartly across the face with a loud smack. Guy
clutches his head and Dave applauds loudly.*

GUY
Careless bugger. Could have had me eye out.

GERALD
Carry on everyone. Sorry, mate, sorry. Now for the
socks.

Guy staggers off to join Nathan.

NATHAN
Bet that never happened to Bobby Charlton.

*Dave is having trouble with the sock part of the routine. In
an effort to reach his feet, he begins to totter and wobble. The
sock won't come off without tremendous tugging. The routine
breaks up in disarray. Nathan switches off the music.*

That were crap.

GERALD
Give it a chance. Bet even Madonna has a job taking off
her socks.

*Over by one of the machines, Gaz rips down the seam of a
pair of Lomper's security guard trousers.*

LOMPER
What you doing wi' them, you gert bugger? They're
bloody borrowed.

GAZ

Keep your hair on, Lomps. We need 'em for the do. It's
what they do. Velcro down the seam, then bingo, all is
revealed. I'll sew 'em back up after.

LOMPER

Yeah right, and when did you turn into an ace sewer
then?

NATHAN

Prison.

*There is an awkward silence as everyone realises this is not a
joke.*

GAZ

Cheers, Nat.

EXT. WORKING MEN'S CLUB. DAY

*Gaz and Nathan are remonstrating with Alan, the gnarly
owner of the working men's club. Alan never once breaks his
steady rhythm of loading crates of beer from the street into
the club.*

GAZ

Come on, Al, it's me.

ALAN

And that's precisely why it's a hundred quid up front.
Half price. You book me club for nowt, you don't turn
up – give me back word – and I'm left with an empty bar
on a Saturday night. No can do, kid.

GAZ

'Course we'll turn up. Al, I haven't got a hundred
quid . . .

Alan stops loading crates and looks Gaz in the face.

ALAN

If you tell me what you're up to it might help.

GAZ
(after a long pause)
I can't. Top secret.

ALAN

Sorry, youth.

INT. FACTORY. DAY

On the shop floor, Mandy is overseeing a line of Women who are automatically snapping the arms of plastic dolls into their torsos. She spots Nathan and Gaz gesturing over the noise of the machines and the radio. She goes over to them and ruffles Nathan's hair.

MANDY

Hiya love.
(to Gaz)
What do you want?

GAZ

Hiya, Mandy, y'alright? Listen, I'm going to get all your money for you – our money – Nathan's – oh you know what I mean. For definite this time.

MANDY

Right, yeah. That all?

GAZ

Thing is, Mand, you have to give out to get back, don't you? In business, like.

MANDY

I'm not sure I'm hearing this.

GAZ

I'll get it all – the whole lot. I just need –

MANDY

– you want some money? I need someone in' packing
section. It's two fifty an hour. You can start now. You
coming?

*Gaz can't even try to explain. Mandy turns on her heel and
walks back to the assembly line.*

INT. BUILDING SOCIETY. DAY

Nathan drags Gaz by the hand into the building society.

GAZ

Nathan, you can't do this, it's your savings, kiddo.

Nathan can barely see over the till.

NATHAN

I can. I just need your signature, don't I? It says in'
book.
                    (*to the Cashier*)
I'd like to take me money out please.

GAZ

Well, you bloody well can't have it.
                    (*to the Cashier*)
You're alright, love, it's sorted.

NATHAN

It's my money. I want it. A hundred pounds, please.

GAZ

Well, when you're eighteen you can walk in here and get
it yourself, can't you?

NATHAN

You said you'd get it back.

GAZ
                    (*reasoning*)
I know, but you don't want to listen to what I say.

83

NATHAN

You *said* so. I believe you.

GAZ

You do?

NATHAN

Yes.

GAZ

Blimey, Nath.

The Cashier looks at Nathan and Gaz, stamps Nathan's book, counts out a hundred pounds and slides it across to Nathan. Nathan solemnly gives it to Gaz.

EXT. SHEFFIELD STREET. DAY

The Gang are walking casually down the street. Gaz looks around and nods his head. Suddenly, Gerald whisks a bucket out from under his parka, Dave slops the wall-paper paste on a hoarding, whilst Lomper slaps up a poster advertising 'Hot Metal's' first appearance. Guy and the Horse lean casually either side to block the view.

GUY

It's not straight.

LOMPER

Give over. It's only a poster.

Down the street come Sheryl and Louise. High-heeled and dangerous, they know Gaz of old.

GAZ

Aye up, gents. This is all we need. Alright, sweethearts?

SHERYL

Garry the lad. What you up to then, Shifty?

GAZ

Bit o' this, bit o' that, bit o' the other.

Louise snatches a poster from under Lomper's coat and eyes it archly.

Just a bit of advertising. For some mates, like.

> SHERYL
> (*not buying it for a second*)
> Oh aye? And whose gonna want to see your 'mates'? We had the real thing up 'ere t'other day.

> GAZ
> (*disconcerted*)
> Well, we – us mates, are better.

> SHERYL
> And how's that then?

> GAZ
> (*searching for inspiration*)
> Well . . . er, this lot go all the way.
> > (*big smile*)
> Don't they, lads?

                              DAVE
                        (*incredulous*)
You what?

                             LOUISE
The full monty? You lot? Hellfire, that *would* be worth a
look. See you there . . .

*Louise and Sheryl wander off giggling. The Gang advance on
Gaz who is backing fast and apologetically up the street.*

                              GAZ
Now just keep your hair on . . .

                             DAVE
                     (*prodding Gaz's chest*)
No way, no and never. In that order, kid.

                             HORSE
No one said owt about going the full monty to *me*.

                              GAZ
You heard 'em. We've got to give 'em summat your
average ten-bob stripper don't. Niche marketing, isn't it?
Read it in a book.

                             HORSE
Yeah but me willy. I mean to say . . .

                            LOMPER
Your willy? What about *my* willy?

                            GERALD
                         (*groaning*)
A laffin' stock. Totally.

                              GAZ
They're coming, aren't they?

                            LOMPER
Aye, wi' a pair of scissors. They known it's us, you know.

GAZ

Yeah and by closing time every bugger in Sheffield's
gonna know it's us whether we do it or we don't. Now
we can either forget it and go back to' sodding Job Club
or do it and just maybe get rich. And I tell you summat,
folks don't laugh so loud when you've a grand in your
back pocket. Now are you in or are you out?

INT. JOB CLUB. DAY

*It looks as if the Gang have thrown in the towel. Gaz,
Lomper, Gerald, Guy and the Horse are lined up miserably
waiting to sign on. Playing on the radio behind the dole
counter is the number in the Gang's routine. In the dole
queue, Gaz detects the faintest stirrings from the Gang. A
shoulder move here, a hand gesture there, a barely noticeable
squeezed buttock. Only the trained eye would notice. The rest
of the dole queue remain morose, preoccupied. Gaz watches,
fascinated. For the Gang it is like trying not to giggle in
church. The urge to dance is bubbling in them. As the song
gets under their skin, their movements synchronise
irrepressibly. Still only the minutest of gestures, nevertheless
these men are cooking with suppressed energy. Then just as
the song reaches its climactic end, Gerald is suddenly at the
head of the queue. His inhibitions snapping, he breaks out
into a full double-shimmy and a shaky 360 twirl, before
slapping his UB 40 on the counter.*

INT. GERALD'S HOUSE. DAY

*Gerald opens the door to be confronted by Lomper, Dave,
Guy and the Horse. Guy is wearing shades, Bermuda shorts
and sandals. Dave and Lomper are in T-shirts. Outside it is
pouring with rain. Guy holds up a bottle of sun tan oil.*

GERALD

No.

Gerald closes the door on them. Guy knocks on the door.

> GUY
> (*off-screen*)
> Gerald? Come on, just an hour, that's all.

A bottle of sun tan oil is waved through the letter-box.

> GUY
> I've brought me own . . .

Gerald opens the door and lets them in.

> GERALD
> *I* shouldn't be here, let alone you bloody beach bums.
> What if Linda comes back? One hour. That's all.

BEDROOM. DAY

*Guy is luxuriating on the sunbed, with nothing on except his
Bermudas and black eye-protectors. Dave studies one of
Linda's* Cosmopolitans *intently. Lomper is going through the
dance steps to himself up and down the bedroom, his eyes
constantly moving to Guy's body, stretched out on the sunbed.*

> DAVE
> Blimey. You get fit birds in here, don't you?

Lomper lomps over to have a look, followed by the Horse.

> LOMPER
> Nah. Tits too big.

> HORSE
> Yeh? I didn't know they could be.

> GERALD
> D'you mind, you?

*Gerald has just spotted Lomper rifling through Linda's
cosmetics on the dressing table.*

LOMPER

Anti-wrinkle cream? Does it work on fellas an' all?

DAVE

(*pointedly*)

Well I just pray they're more understanding about us, that's all.

HORSE

You what?

DAVE

Well they're gonna be looking at us like that, aren't they? Eh? What if, next Saturday, four hundred women turn round and say, 'He's too fat.' 'He's too old' and 'He' –
(*pointing at Lomper*)
'is a pigeon-chested little tosser.' What happens then, eh?

Lomper ceases to dance. Guy pulls his protective eye-shades up, suddenly alert.

HORSE

(*appalled*)

They wouldn't say that. Would they?

DAVE

Why the chuff not? *He's* just said her tits are too big.

LOMPER

That's different. We're . . .
(*shrugging*)
men . . .

DAVE

And?

GERALD

(*suddenly generous*)

Well I think she's got nice tits, actually.

LOMPER
(*defensive*)
I never said owt about her personality, like. She's
probably right nice if you get to know her.

DAVE
No, and they won't say nowt about your personality,
neither. Which is good. 'Cos you're basically a bastard.
Bollocks to your personality, they've come to look at
this, haven't they?
(*points at himself*)
And I tell you, mate, anti-wrinkle cream there may be.
But anti-fat-bastard cream there is none.

*There is a thoughtful silence, Guy gets off the sunbed and
reaches into his beach bag.*

GUY
Lads it might not be such a good time for this but –

*Guy brings out a handful of red leather thongs from his bag.
The Gang examine them with a mixture of awe and terror.*

DAVE
(*distressed*)
Oh Mother . . .

GUY
(*apologetic*)
Gaz said summat a bit flash, y'know.
(*encouraging*)
They're top of the range. Real leather, like.

DAVE
Yeah, but . . .

LOMPER
Don't get much for your money, do you?

                    HORSE
                   (*quietly*)
What's today again?

                    GERALD
Monday.

                    LOMPER
And when are we on?

                    GERALD
Friday. Dress rehearsal, Tuesday.

                    DAVE
Undress rehearsal.

                    HORSE
I think I'm gonna be sick.

EXT. SHEFFIELD STREET. EVENING

*In a phone-box the Horse is cradling the receiver furtively
near his mouth while glancing up and down the street.*

                    HORSE
How can I read the instructions? There weren't any . . .
No. Maybe there's a part missing . . . Just a minute.

*The Horse delves into an Adidas bag and pulls out bits of
what can only be a vacuum-operated penis enlarger. He goes
through a check list, dubiously fitting together each strange
part of the machine.*

Yep, yeah, yeah, got that . . . if that's what you call it . . .
Well if it's all there, how come it's not working . . .?
What d'you mean 'in what sense'?

*A middle aged Woman peers into the phone-box. The Horse
shoves the enlarger back into the bag, gestures angrily at the
phone and turns his back on the Woman.*

HORSE
(*whispering*)
It's not working in the sense that it's not *working*. No I
can't speak up. Nothing's happening, know what I'm
saying? Nothing's getting bigger . . . It's an emergency, is
this.

*The Woman has been joined by another Woman. Fascinated,
they listen in.*

(*agitated*)
I dunno, what d'you want me to do, get a ruler out an'
start measuring up in' bloody phone-box? You tell me,
mate.

*At this suggestion, the two Women look at each other in
horrified delight.*

Placid? Oh 'flaccid', right . . . How many? Right. And
what about – the other – not flaccid?
(*surprised*)
Really? Sure that's normal, roughly, like . . .? Well, *I'm*
normal then. How about that?

*The Horse puts down the phone, too absorbed in his own joy
to notice the incongruity of the applause that has broken out
from the listening Women outside. He struts out of the phone-
box a new man.*

Did you hear that? Eh?

*Then the Horse suddenly remembers that this is perhaps not
the sort of good news to share with everyone.*

D'you mind? Private phone-call were that.

He hastens down the street to the laughter of the Women.

INT. DAVE'S BEDROOM. NIGHT

*Dave walks into the room wearing his pyjama bottoms. He
stands next to the bed, looking miserable.*

JEAN
Come in and cuddle up, then.

Dave gets into the bed and cuddles up close to Jean. Soon they are kissing.

What's up, Big Man, eh?

DAVE
Nothing. Nothing at all.

Dave gets on top of Jean and begins to make love. But almost as soon as he has started, he gives up and sits on the edge of the bed.

JEAN
Dave? Dave . . .

DAVE
Sorry.

INT. DAVE'S BEDROOM. LATER. NIGHT

In her night dress. Jean looks out of the window at the light from the shed. Inside, she can see a figure moving around.

INT. DAVE'S SHED. NIGHT

Dave moves his Pirelli calendar aside and retrieves a Mars Bar hidden behind it. He takes the wrapper off and takes a bite. Fishing in his hold-all, he brings out a roll of cling film. Pulling up his sweatshirt, he proceeds with difficulty to wrap the cling film round and round his huge stomach. He sits there, cling-filmed and chewing.

INT. GAZ'S HOUSE. NIGHT

Gaz is going through his dance steps in the kitchen. He is too preoccupied to notice Nathan coming downstairs. He watches critically as the song finishes – fractionally after Gaz does.

NATHAN

You're ahead.

GAZ

You're supposed to be in bed. This tape deck's slow.
Always has been.

Gaz takes a swig of beer from a can on the side-board.

NATHAN

You'll get fat.

GAZ
(*his nerves showing*)
Give us a striping break, will you?

NATHAN

Sorry.

GAZ

Nath, tell us straight, kid. We're not just making the
biggest arses of ourselves in the known universe, are we?

*After a pause, Nathan goes over to the tape deck and presses
rewind.*

NATHAN

Give it another go, eh?

EXT. BUS STOP. MORNING

*Hunched into his jacket, Dave is sitting in a bus shelter
overlooking Sheffield, trying to coax some life into a roll-up. A
troubled-looking Gerald joins Dave.*

GERALD

Not such a bad morning, is it?

*Dave, frost-bitten and trying to relight his cigarette against
the wind's fierce buffeting, gives Gerald a strange look.*

Dave mate, can I have a word? Private like.

DAVE

S'pose so, yeah.

GERALD
(*after a long pause*)
That's the new Olympic pool down there, isn't it? You
ever been swimming? Can't swim, me. Dave, you won't
tell anyone about this.

DAVE
(*looking around him*)
Your secret's safe wi' me, mate.

GERALD
When I were twelve year old us school took us to
swimming lessons. Mixed classes, you know. Boys. And
girls.

*Gerald looks across at Dave, hoping he has said enough for
Dave to understand. Dave raises his eyes, puzzled.*

It were terrible, Dave. I were there, standing at' side o'
pool in me trunks with all these pretty lasses around in
bikinis, and well, I got a –
(*gesturing*)
– *you know.*

DAVE
(*not knowing*)
Oh. An *I know.*

GERALD

Do you?

DAVE
(*losing patience*)
No, Gerald, I bloody don't.

GERALD

You know, a . . .

Gerald waves at his crotch. Dave finally clicks.

> DAVE
> Oh. So what did you do?

> GERALD
> Jumped in' deep end, didn't I?

> DAVE
> Thought you couldn't swim.

> GERALD
> Couldn't. Nearly fucking drowned.

Gerald grabs Dave's sleeve desperately.

> But what if it happens again? Eh? Think of that. In front
> of four hundred women . . . I'd have to chuffin'
> emigrate.

*With uncharacteristic violence, Dave shakes off Gerald's hand
and stands up.*

> DAVE
> Gerald, you're talking to' wrong man.

Dave throws his cigarette away and strides down the road.

> GERALD
> Dave? Dave, you'll miss' bus.

But Dave keeps on walking.

EXT. SHEFFIELD. DAY

*Side by side, five figures stride purposefully up the road: Gaz,
Nathan, Horse, Lomper and Gerald. Men with a mission,
they fail to notice the police car parked in an alley near the
rolling mill*

INT. POLICE CAR. DAY

Inside the car, a Policeman is absorbed in dive-bombing a

*polystyrene cup of coffee with a sweetener dispenser. Making
the appropriate aeroplane noises as he goes, he zooms high
over the cup and drops a sweetener into the coffee.*

> POLICEMAN
> Bombs gone, returning to base . . . Ah, roger that,
> Squadron Leader.

*The Policeman puts the dispenser into a steep climb. As he
does so, he notices the five figures striding by. Putting the
coffee on the dashboard, he starts the engine and cruises
slowly out of the alley after them.*

INT. ROLLING MILL. DAY

*Sitting rather bemusedly on a battered sofa in the middle of
the rolling mill is the Horse's Mum with two equally ancient
cronies and a couple of small babies in tow.*

*In the shower room, the Gang are changing into their quick-
release security guard trousers and putting on hats and ties.
Acute tension hangs in the air. Gaz paces around fretfully.
Gerald is peering out of the doorway at the audience whilst
the Horse rubs baby oil into his shoulders and back.*

> GERALD
> (*fretfully*)
> I thought you said just your mum.

> HORSE
> They're family, what can you do?

*Beryl, a deeply dark and beautiful woman sashays sexily up to
the sofa where the Horse's Mum is sitting.*

> GERALD
> Who the hellfire's that?

                         HORSE
                      (*horrified*)
It's Beryl. My niece.

                         NATHAN
                       (*to Gaz*)
Where's Dave?

                          GAZ
He'll be here.

                         NATHAN
Has anyone seen Dave?

Gerald suddenly looks around guiltily.

                          GAZ
I said he'll be here.

                         NATHAN
Alright, alright, only asking . . .

                         GERALD
Gaz, I think I said summat out of order to him at the
bus-stop. He got the hump and pissed off.

                          GAZ
Gerald, you berk . . .

                         GERALD
Sorry.

*Gaz strides towards the exit. In the background, watched by
Lomper, Guy can be seen running full pelt towards the wall.
This time he gets one leg really high and head first, crashes to
the floor.*

INT. WOOLWORTHS. DAY

*Dressed in his security guard's uniform, Dave is leaning
against the pick 'n' mix bins. Clumsily he tries to juggle a few
Quality Street which inevitably fall on the floor. He bends to*

pick them up and as he straightens, spots Gaz leaning against the display, chewing a toffee, arms folded, staring at him.

> GAZ
>
> What you doing, Dave?

> DAVE
>
> What's it look like?

> GAZ
>
> We're on in three days' time for chuff's sake. Where. The fuck. Are you?

> DAVE
>
> I'm here. Working, earning, not pissing about. That's where. End of chat.

Dave turns and walks away from Gaz. Gaz follows him.

INT. STEELWORKS STORE AREA. DAY

Horse's Mum has got her knitting out. Nathan looks fretfully at his watch.

> GUY
>
> Where are they?

> NATHAN
>
> Don't look at me.

> GERALD
>
> They're disappearing one by one like summat out of an Agatha fuckin' Christie. Horse, mate, get out front and tell 'em we've got a delay on.

> HORSE
>
> They won't wait for ever.

Outside, Horse's Mum begins a slow hand clap.

INT. WOOLWORTHS. DAY

Gaz follows Dave into the suit section.

GAZ

Well come on then, Mr Security, do your job.

Gaz rips a suit off the nearest hanger and heads for the door at speed. Dave goes after him.

DAVE

Gaz . . . please don't, please.

GAZ

You've got a job, do it.

DAVE

Gazza . . .

EXT. WOOLWORTHS. DAY

Gaz makes it through the doors with the suit, setting off all the alarms in the process. He laughs manically, shouting and waving the suit in the air, with Dave close behind.

GAZ

Keep up, you fat bastard.

Gaz tries to dodge around a shopping trolley, slowing him enough for Dave to grab him. He hauls Gaz upright. Dave shakes him hard.

DAVE

Don't call me a fat bastard. Ever. Alright? Alright?

Dave stops shaking him.

GAZ

I need you, Dave. Can't do it without you, can I? You're a mate.

Dave stares at him long and hard, then releases his grip and lets Gaz go. Gaz straightens his clothes up in an attempt at dignity.

                              DAVE
Sorry. I can't. I – just can't. Better leg it.

Gaz holds out the suit to Dave.

                              GAZ
Here. It's bad enough *one* of us dressed like a fucking
king penguin.

Gaz turns and walks off into the crowd.

                              DAVE
See you about, eh?

INT. STEELWORKS. ROOM OFF STORE AREA. DAY

Horse and Guy are attempting to comfort a troubled Gerald.

                            GERALD
I'd be alright if we could just get on wi' it. It's the
bloody waiting that scares me.

                             HORSE
Listen, just think about the most boring thing you can
come up with. That'll keep it all well in order.

                            GERALD
Like what?

                              GUY
Double glazing salesmen.

                             HORSE
Gardening. The Queen's speech.

                              GUY
Dire Straits' double album. Nature programmes.

                            GERALD
I like nature programmes.

                              GUY
Yes but they don't give you a hard on, do they?

(*thinking*)
Do they? Blimey, Gerald.

                        GERALD
Shurrup you, it's not funny. It's medical.

Gaz appears.

                        LOMPER
So where is he?

                        GAZ
He's not coming.

The Gang are nonplussed.

                        NATHAN
You what?

                        GAZ
You heard . . . We can do without him. No problem,
alright? Lets get the fuckin' show on the road.

                        NATHAN
But what about Dave?

                        GAZ
(*viciously*)
Nothing about Dave.

*There is a shocked pause. Then, clapping his hands
authoritatively, the Horse takes charge.*

                        HORSE
Come on, lads, let's go, let's go.

INT. STEELWORKS. STORE AREA. DAY

*To thumping music, the Gang take the floor. They make a
tentative start, Gaz's anger at Dave is still written on his face.
He glances over to where Nathan is controlling the stereo and
sharply motions him to turn up the volume. And with the*

music pumped up, the Gang really being to cook. The Horse's Mum stops knitting, Beryl is wide-eyed and the rest of the spectators look genuinely impressed – and not a little surprised – as the Gang strut their stuff.

EXT. STEELWORKS. DAY

A stream of uniformed and plain-clothes Policemen jump out of the back of a police van and surround the rolling mill.

INT. STEELWORKS. STORE AREA. DAY

The Gang whip off their quick-release trousers, revealing fine red thongs. Which is, of course, the moment the Police charge into the mill from all sides.

> POLICEMAN
> (*through a loud-hailer*)
> Everyone stay where they are.

Nathan cuts the music dead. The Gang freeze mid step, the Horse covering a naked nipple. Only Guy is quick enough to tap Lomper on the shoulder and nod towards the fire escape.

EXT. ROLLING MILL. DAY

The Gang, minus Guy and Lomper are being led one by one into the back of a police van by some amused Policemen. As they climb in, two tiny naked figures can be seen sprinting along the roof of the rolling mill. Unnoticed, they speed from one side of the frame to the other and disappear.

INT. POLICE STATION. DAY

Covered only in silver foil emergency blankets, the Horse, Gerald and Gaz are standing in line at the charge desk. Behind the desk, a bemused Duty Sergeant is aiming sweeteners from a great height into his tea – obviously a station obsession. Gaz keeps looking over his shoulder to where Nathan is being questioned by two over-friendly Social Workers.

> GAZ
> We were dancing alright then an' all.

> GERALD
> (*miserable*)
> Me feet are cold.

> SOCIAL WORKER
> So your daddy dances in front of you, does he?

> NATHAN
> When he's rehearsing, like.

> SOCIAL WORKER
> And does he ever – do things, Nathan?

> NATHAN
> Like what?

> SOCIAL WORKER
> Does he, well, ever take his clothes off, for instance?

> NATHAN
> Wouldn't be much point if he didn't, would there?

The Social Workers exchange meaningful looks.

EXT. BACK GARDEN. DAY

His mouth full of clothes pegs, a middle-aged Man is standing in the garden hanging washing on the line. He is halfway through pegging up a dressing-gown when a baby begins crying inside the house. The Man's eyes narrow and he goes into the house. Suddenly, Lomper and Guy leap the fence and begin tearing down the washing. Guy only manages to get the dressing-gown before there is a yell from the house.

> GUY
> Come on, Lomps for Christ's sake.

*Guy vaults the fence and Lomper grabs a sheet before
following him. The Man charges out of the house in time to
see the two giggling figures hurdling a series of back-garden
fences, Lomper's white sheet billowing like a cape behind him.*

INT. POLICE INTERVIEW ROOM. DAY

*Gaz, Gerald and the Horse sit in their space blankets. They
have been joined by Nathan. Intrigued, the Police Inspector is
interviewing them.*

INSPECTOR
Come on then, amaze me.

GAZ
Told you. Robbing pipes. That's all.

GERALD
Eh?

GAZ
(*vicious whisper*)
Well which would *you* prefer?

INSPECTOR
Robbing pipes? Garry, my friend, no bugger robs pipes
in the buff.

GAZ
(*confident smile*)
We do. Don't get your clothes dirty, do you?

INSPECTOR
Well don't fret, gents, there's a reet good laundry in
Wakefield Prison.

GERALD
(*appalled*)
Eh?

Another Policeman enters carrying a stack of video tapes.

POLICEMAN
Security camera tapes off the front desk.

INSPECTOR
So what happened to the security guard?

POLICEMAN
Vanished, leaving nowt but, er, half his trousers.

INSPECTOR
Half?

The Policeman shrugs.

INSPECTOR
Well, we'd better have a look, hadn't we, gents?

HORSE
(*resigned*)
Here we go.

INT. POLICE INTERVIEW ROOM. DAY

Gaz, Gerald, the Horse and the Inspector are sitting watching the TV screen. Behind them the room is crowded with the rest of the police station, all leering in through the door. Except for the Gang, the room is in good-natured uproar. On the TV, captured by the security cameras, is the Gang's whole dance routine, including the raid.

GERALD
(*to the Inspector*)
Do you mind a sec?

Gerald leans forward, presses rewind and turns to Gaz accusingly.

GERALD
I told you – look, you're always ahead here. Watch.

GAZ
You're always bloody behind, more like.

Forgetting where he is now his professionalism has been called into question, Gerald turns to the crowd of Police.

> GERALD
>
> Look, shurrup, will you?

The crowd of Police fall silent. The video plays through.

> INSPECTOR
>
> He's right. You're ahead.

> GAZ
> *(annoyed)*
>
> Oh go bollocks.

EXT. ROOFTOPS SHEFFIELD. EVENING

Lomper and Guy are perched on top of Lomper's garage. Giggling still, Lomper slides open the window to his bedroom.

> LOMPER
>
> Please, no, shurrup now. Me mum, for Christ's sake.

> GUY
>
> Not a word, I promise. I've always wanted to meet your mum.

INT. LOMPER'S HOUSE. EVENING

Lomper drops into his room through the window. Guy starts to follow and gets hung up on the dressing-gown halfway.

> GUY
>
> Well give us a hand. Can't get me arms through.

Lomper holds him around the thighs as Guy squeezes his arms through. He is down to his leather thong again. Lomper gently lowers him to the floor, Guy's arms around his shoulders. Suddenly the two near-naked men become aware of the sexuality of their position. Guy tries to break an atmosphere laden with sexual tension.

(*full volume*)
Made it!

Panic-struck, Lomper clamps a hand over Guy's mouth and nods towards the door and the direction of his mother.

LOMPER

Shh . . . dozy bastard.

Both stand motionless, still holding onto each other, listening for Lomper's Mum's footsteps. Silence. Gently, Guy takes Lomper's hand from his mouth. Their faces are close together. They stare at each other for a long moment, a hair's breadth away from kissing.

Summat's wrong.

Lomper breaks away and goes to the door. Guy looks bereft, utterly abandoned.

LOMPER

Mother? Mother?

Lomper goes out of the door.

(*off-screen*)

Mum . . .!

The sound of Lomper's feet thundering down the stairs.

INT. LOMPER'S HOUSE. EVENING

Lomper crouches at the bottom of the stairs by the crumpled shape of his Mum. He strokes her bare arm as Guy stands motionless at the top of the stairs.

LOMPER
(*quietly*)

Silly cow, silly bloody cow.

Gently untangling the dressing-gown, the naked son lifts his

*mother into his arms and carries the limp figure into her
bedroom.*

INT. BEDROOM. EVENING

*With great tenderness, Lomper lays her out on the bed and
stands beside it, holding her old hand and stroking the back of
it with his thumb. Guy stands watching, holding himself
around the shoulders, shivering slightly. He turns and quietly
goes out, shutting the door gently behind him.*

INT. POLICE STATION. EVENING

*Carrying a pile of clothes, the Duty Sergeant enters the
reception area of the station where the Gang are sat wearing
their blankets. Gerald sifts through the clothes and hands
some jeans to Gaz who is busy remonstrating with the Duty
Sergeant at the charge desk.*

> GAZ
> What d'you mean I can't bloody see him. He's me son.
> I've been charged with nowt, me – ask Smiler in there –
> no charges . . .

> DUTY SERGEANT
> Sorry. The Social Services have requested an interview
> with you before your son can be returned to your care.

> GAZ
> (*struggling into his jeans*)
> Well here I am. Interview me, go on. Try me, ask me
> owt. Starter for ten.

> DUTY SERGEANT
> Not me, mate, them. Have to make an appointment.

> GAZ
> Halle-bloody-luja . . .

Suddenly the door opens and Mandy walks in. The Horse

quickly pulls on his trousers. Ignoring Gaz completely, Mandy addresses the Duty Sergeant.

> MANDY
>
> I've come to pick up my son

> DUTY SERGEANT
>
> Right. Just a minute, madam.

The Duty Sergeant disappears.

> GAZ
>
> Listen, Mandy, it's fine, we've not been charged or owt . . .

> MANDY
>
> So this is your great money-making enterprise is it, Garry? Pornography.

> GAZ
>
> Don't be daft. I were getting you your money that's all.

> MANDY
>
> *My* money? Nathan's money.

The Duty Sergeant returns with Nathan who is enjoying wearing the Duty Sergeant's hat.

> GAZ
>
> Nathan, you alright, kid?

> NATHAN
>
> Yeah, fine. Hi, Mum.

> MANDY
> (*whipping the hat off*)
>
> Come on, Nathan, we're going now.

> NATHAN
>
> I'm with dad this weekend.

> MANDY
>
> Change of plan, love.

Mandy turns to Gaz who is still struggling into his jeans.

Unemployed, criminal record, maintenance arrears of seven hundred pounds, now arrest for indecent exposure. Still think you're a suitable father, do you?

NATHAN

He's trying.

GAZ
(*himself surprised*)

See.

MANDY

Bit late for that.

Mandy takes Nathan by the hand and walks out of the door. Gaz staggers to the door, getting caught up in his half-on trousers.

GAZ

Hang on a minute . . .

MANDY

Look at yourself, Gary. Just look at yourself.

Mandy and Nathan walk down the street.

GAZ

See you soon, eh, kid? Thumbs up.
(*appealing to Gerald*)
She can't do this, can she? I've not been charged. I'm trying, aren't I? He said. You heard him.

Gerald, the Horse and the Duty Sergeant's look on silently. After a pause, the Horse says gently.

HORSE

I think you've got me jeans on, mate.

INT. CAFF DAY

Dave is tucking into an all-day breakfast, free now of all dietary constraints. He wipes the juices from the plate with a piece of bread and is about to put it in his mouth, when he notices a man opposite reading the paper. The front page reads: 'SHEFFIELD STRIPPERS EXPOSED – PHOTOS'.

EXT. STREET/NEWSAGENT. EVENING

Gerald walks out of a newsagent's carrying thirty copies of the Yorkshire Evening Post. *He looks both ways before dumping them in the bin and hurrying on. Then, his vanity getting the better of him, Gerald comes back, tears out one of the photos, gives it an approving once-over, stuffs it in his wallet and walks off.*

EXT. GERALD'S HOUSE. EVENING

Turning the corner, Gerald is confronted by a removals van in front of his house. He breaks into a run and arrives at his garden gate in time to witness two Removal Men man-handling the sunbed out of the door. Linda stands in the garden, watching, holding one of the garden gnomes in her hands. Hopelessly, Gerald joins her.

> LINDA

So.

> GERALD

Yeah.

> LINDA

And this has been going on how long?

> GERALD

Six months. Nearly.

LINDA
(*matter of fact*)
Six months. Six months.

Very deliberately, Linda lets the gnome fall onto the path. It smashes.

I can cope with losing the sunbed, the car, the television. I can even cope with the shame of everyone watching *this*. But what I find hard, what I find very hard, Gerald, is that you never said. Six months. Six bloody months and you never said a word. Not a word to your wife. What does that make me, Gerald?

Gerald can only shake his head. An armchair is carried past them.

Have you got somewhere to sleep tonight? Wherever it is you go when you're 'at work'?

Gerald nods. He stares at the gnome.

GERALD
I thought you liked them.

LINDA
No, Gerald. I've never liked them.

Gerald walks off down the street.

INT. DOLE OFFICE. DAY

The Horse comes to the front of the queue to sign on. The Woman behind the counter taps in his details onto the computer.

WOMAN
(*automatically*)
Have you been actively seeking work for the last two weeks?

HORSE

Yeah.

WOMAN

Done any work, paid or unpaid, during the last two
weeks?

HORSE

No.

*The Woman peers over the top of her glasses with just a hint
of a smile.*

WOMAN

That's not what I heard.

INT./EXT. GAZ'S HOUSE. EVENING

*Gaz is sitting miserably in his bare living room when there is
a knock at the door. Gaz opens the door to find Gerald
holding a bag of chips.*

GERALD

They've took me sunbed. They've took bloody
everything.

GAZ

Kept hold of your chips, though. Brew on.

*Gaz holds the door open for Gerald. He walks in holding up
a letter.*

GERALD

Registered bankrupt, house repossessed, wife thrown me
out. And guess what? I've just been offered a job.

GAZ
(*deadpan*)

Congratulations.

INT. DAVE'S HOUSE. EVENING

Dave walks into the house. At the bottom of the stairs stands a suitcase.

> DAVE
> Jean? Jean, love?

No reply. Puzzled, Dave puts his head around the kitchen door, sees there is no one around and goes upstairs.

INT. BEDROOM. EVENING

Jean is sitting on the bed when Dave walks in.

> DAVE
> There you are. Not such a bad first day.

Jean looks up at Dave, then holds up a bottle of posh aftershave.

> JEAN
> I should have guessed when you started wearing this poof-juice. You never put it on for me, did you?

> DAVE
> Jean . . .

Jean holds up Dave's red leather thong distastefully.

> JEAN
> But this . . . Never thought you were up for that sort of caper, David. That explains a few things at least.

> DAVE
> No, Jean. I know it don't look good but –

> JEAN
> – bloody right it don't. All them times you were late back. And silly cow here thought you were looking for a job. No wonder. No bloody wonder –

(laughs)
– it's so obvious.

DAVE

No, honest, I were with Gaz.

JEAN

Oh, one of Gaz's little tarts, is she? Yeah, she'd have to
be to like this sort of . . . shit.

Jean throws the thong at Dave and makes for the door.

DAVE
(shouting)
Shut up a minute, will you? It's nowt to do with any
fucking women, alright?

Jean stops in the doorway.

I'm – I were a stripper, right? Me and Gaz and some
fellas. Though we could make a bob or two taking us
clothes off.

JEAN

Strippers.

DAVE

Alright, alright, I know.

JEAN

You. And Gaz? Strippers.

DAVE

We weren't *that* bad.

*Dave performs a perfect, if lack-lustre, twirl. Jean raises her
eyebrows, impressed.*

Been practising. Only I couldn't, could I?

JEAN

Why?

DAVE

Because.

JEAN

Because what?

DAVE

Well look at me.

JEAN

So?

DAVE

Jeanie, who wants to see *this* dance?

JEAN

Me, Dave. I do.

Jean gets off the bed and walks up to Dave. She puts her head on his massive stomach and wraps her arms around him.

EXT. SCHOOL. DAY

With a football under his arm, Gaz and Gerald loiter by the school gates as a stream of children pour out from classes. Gaz spots Nathan.

GAZ

Alright, Nath.

Seeing his father, Nathan's face brightens.

NATHAN

Hiya.

As Nathan approaches, Barry and Mandy walk down the path to meet him.

GAZ

Fancy a kick around in' park?

MANDY

Just in time, love.

118

Nathan's eyes move between the two groups. He stops. A surge of children push past and around him.

(*to Gaz*)
You shouldn't be here.

GAZ

Say who?

BARRY

Read the lawyer's letter, why don't you?

Gaz turns to Barry. Odds on, he'll hit him.

NATHAN

We're going swimming, Dad. Wanna come?

This brings Gaz up short.

GAZ

Can't kid. Haven't brought me trunks, have I?

NATHAN

We could get 'em, couldn't we, Mum?

GAZ

No, I can't, love.

NATHAN

Why?

GAZ

I just – well I just can't. Sorry.

NATHAN
(*to Mandy*)
He's not allowed, is he?

MANDY

Come on, love.

Mandy looks as distraught as Gaz, but she just turns, takes hold of Nathan's hand and disappears with the crowd of children. Gaz is left watching Nathan go. Gerald puts an arm around Gaz's shoulders. At this moment, the Roller-blader appears, heading at speed down one of the steep streets. There is a split-second's realisation on the Roller-blader's face that the street becomes cobbled before his blades hit them. There is a spectacular wipe-out. Bloodied, the Roller-blader gets to his knees. Gaz turns to Gerald.

GAZ

See. It's not all bad.

INT. WOOLWORTHS. DAY

Dave is patrolling the store when suddenly, a rack of coats speaks.

GAZ
(*off-screen*)
Dave . . . Oi, you deaf git.

Dave doesn't even bother to investigate, content to talk to the tweed coats and the pair of trainers sticking out of the bottom.

DAVE
What do you want now? I've told you, I'm finished wi' it.

GAZ
(*off-screen*)
We're all finished wi' it, Dave. Just keepin' me 'ead down. I'm a bloody marked man now. In every sodding paper.

DAVE
Sorry about your Nathan. Bad 'un is that.

GAZ
(*off-screen*)
It's Lomper.

DAVE

What does that pasty-faced chuffer want?

GAZ
(*off-screen*)

His mum died two days since.

DAVE
(*brought up short*)

Oh . . . poor lad, I'm sorry.

GAZ
(*off-screen*)

You couldn't borrow us a, you know – jacket or summat
for the funeral, could you?

DAVE

Gaz . . .

GAZ
(*off-screen*)

Oh come on, Dave, it's not for me, is it? It's a
funeral . . .

DAVE
(*pondering then deciding*)

What colour?

GAZ
(*off-screen*)

Orange.

DAVE

Orange?

GAZ
(*off-screen*)

Black, you *knob-'ead*.

DAVE

Oh aye. Hang on.

Dave disappears and returns with two black jackets.

GAZ
(off-screen)
Nice one.

DAVE
Come on then.

Bemused, Gaz comes out of hiding and follows Dave through the shop.

GAZ
Got time off, or what?

DAVE
Nah. That fuckin' pick 'n' mix were driving me crazy. Besides, it's a funeral.

They are approaching the exit. Dave looks across at Gaz.

You ready?

GAZ
Ready when you are, Dave mate.

Shooting the cuffs on their new jackets, the pair walk side by side through the exit, not even breaking step as every alarm in the building goes off.

EXT. GRAVEYARD. DAY

The Gang and almost the whole of the Steelworks Brass Band stand by the side at the grave as the vicar reads the final lines of the funeral service. As he finishes, Lomper raises his trumpet to his trembling lips and tries to play. Nothing happens. He wipes his lips violently on his sleeve, trying to force them to stay in control, and puts the instrument to his lips once more. Again, nothing. Lomper shakes his head and drops the trumpet to his side. There is a bit of awkward shuffling amongst the mourners, then Guy walks up to him,

*whispers something in his ear and squeezes his hand. Lomper
smiles wanly, puts the trumpet to his lips for a third time.
Thinly at first, then with increasing confidence 'Abide with
Me' floats across the graveyard. The music swells as the rest of
the band join in.*

EXT. GRAVEYARD ROAD. DAY

*Facing away from the graveyard, Gaz and Dave are propped
up against Lomper's motor having a roll-up. The last of the
mourners from the band come past. Gaz is fiddling with the
wing-mirror, trying to get a surreptitious look at Guy and
Lomper who are the only ones left by the graveside a hundred
yards away.*

> GAZ
> They bloody are, you know. They're holding hands.

> DAVE
> They never.

> GAZ
> Straight up.

> DAVE
> (*shoving Gaz out of the way*)
> Gis a look. I don't even hold hands with ruddy *lasses*,
> me.
> (*suddenly thinking*)
> Maybe I should . . . Who'd of bloody thought it,
> though? Aye well, nowt as queer as folk.

*Gaz chokes on his roll-up. Then Dave realises what he has
said and a fit of laughter takes hold.*

> (*incredibly pleased with himself*)
> Hey, Gaz, I said – nowt as queer as folk.

GAZ
(*failing to suppress his own laughter*)
Shurrup, Dave . . . it's a chuffin' funeral.

*Which only makes Dave's booming laugh worse. The Vicar,
Guy and Lomper and the last of the mourners turn and stare
at this sacrilegious noise. Trying to make amends, Dave gives
them a big, friendly wave.*

DAVE
Sorry!

EXT. WORKING MEN'S CLUB. DAY

*Gaz wanders down the street playing with Nathan's yo-yo as
he goes. A couple of Men rolling a huge tractor tyre down the
street pass him. They start singing 'The Stripper' in obvious
mockery.*

GAZ
Go get shagged.

*Gaz gives the tyre a shove that sends it free-wheeling down
the steep street. Once started, a tyre that size is hard to stop.*

MAN
You bugger . . .

*The two Men set off in pursuit. As Gaz passes the working
men's club, Alan comes out.*

ALAN
Oi, Patricia the Stripper, where you bloody been?

GAZ
What's it to you?

ALAN
Well, what's going on? I've had to buy in twenty barrels
and I've heard not a peep from you.

                              GAZ
Well I hope they're sale or return.

                              ALAN
Joking. You're bloody famous.

                              GAZ
                            (*wincing*)
Don't remind me.

                              ALAN
Aye, I've shifted two hundred odd tickets.

INT. JOB CLUB. DAY

*Dave, Guy and the Horse are sitting morosely in the Job
Club. Gerald, in a new suit, is shaking hands with the Job
Club Manager.*

                     JOB CLUB MANAGER
Good luck, Gerald, all the best.
                         (*to the others*)
Example for you, there.

Gerald joins the Gang. They give him half-hearted whistles.

                             HORSE
Nice suit, Gerald.

                            GERALD
No touching, it's new. I'll keep in touch, like. Never
know, might be some jobs going for you boys.

Suddenly Gaz spins in.

                              GAZ
Lads, we're on. We're bloody on.

                            GERALD
What do you mean?

                              GAZ
Two hundred tickets gone. That's two grand already.

                            HORSE
Nice one.

                            GERALD
Ah, it's a bit late for that now, Gaz. It were a laugh and
all, but you know, fresh start an' all that.

                              GAZ
One more time, Gerald. You've got the rest of your
fucking life to wear a suit, man . . .

*Gerald fingers his new collar, thinking. The Gang wait for a
decision.*

                            GERALD
Just once. That's all.

                              GUY
I'll get Lomps, you sort out the costumes.

Guy rushes outs.

                            HORSE
Three hundred and fifty quid a piece.

                              GAZ
Could be as much as four hundred.

                            DAVE
He'll be back.

*The Gang turn to Dave, who has been sitting quietly
watching the Gang's growing excitement.*

                            GERALD
You what?

                            DAVE
He's gonna regret that.

GAZ

Least he's got the bottle. What do you say, Dave? Are you in? Come on, mate.

The Job Club Manager leans his head out of his office.

JOB CLUB MANAGER

Mr Horsfall.

Dave is torn. He looks to the Manager, then back at Gaz and the Gang.

DAVE

Sorry, lads.

Dave walks to join the Manager.

CUT TO:

INT. WORKING MEN'S CLUB. NIGHT

The hall is packed with chattering, giggling Women. Worse than that, the hall is also packed with Men. Chants of 'Here we go, here we go' break out from various corners of the audience.

INT. BACKSTAGE. NIGHT

Dressed in their security guard uniforms, the Gang are crowded around Gaz nervously in the wings. Gerald's shoulders are being massaged with baby oil by the Horse while Lomper sucks the mouth-piece of his cornet. Only Alan seems to be enjoying the situation. The reason becomes clear. Of all people, it is Gaz who is having problems. Sat down, he is jiggling his legs and is sweating, apparently unaware of Guy massaging his shoulders. Gaz has got total stage fright.

GAZ

Women only, you tosser, women only . . . it's on all' posters for fuck's sake.

ALAN

Nope. No one told me.

GAZ

All' blokes from' pub are there, the bastards.

GERALD

You'll be fine, mate. Once you're on stage –

GAZ

'Once I'm on stage'? What d'you mean 'Once I'm on stage'? I'm going nowhere near that stage. Suicide, that's what it is. Suicide . . . Oh shit . . . I'll give the money back. Alan, announce it. Please?

ALAN
(peering through stage curtains)
To four hundred horny punters? Ask another one, kid. By heck, our old dinner lady's in front row.

The stage resounds to hundreds of feet stamping in increasingly impatient unison.

GAZ

Listen to that for chuff's sake. They're gonna tear us to pieces.

ALAN
(with relish)
They will if you don't get out there, mate. Ever seen a zebra brought down by a pack of wolves? Marvellous them nature films. Marvellous.

GERALD

Brilliant, aren't they?

Guy gives Gerald a leery nudge.

(laughing)
Oh give over.

DAVE

Not lost your bottle, Gaz?

Suddenly Dave and Nathan are standing in front of him.

GAZ

Dave?

DAVE

Well there were nowt on telly, so I thought, give it a go, eh? Found this 'un wandering about outside.

NATHAN

Wouldn't let me in.

GAZ

What the merry hell are you doing here? Your mum'll be throwing a right benny.

NATHAN

She's out front.

GAZ

(*taken aback*)

Is she? That Barry with her, is he?

NATHAN

No, she wouldn't let him come. Said it were ladies only.

GAZ

Nice one, Mand.

ALAN

I can't hold them any longer, kid. Now or never.

With the exception of Gaz, the Gang line up behind the curtains.

HORSE

Can we keep our G-strings on, then Gaz?

GAZ

Perhaps you better had.

DAVE

No you better hadn't. If we're doing it, then just for once, we're doing it right.

INT. WORKING MEN'S CLUB. NIGHT

Alan flicks off a whole bank of switches. Suddenly the club is plunged into darkness. A huge cheer goes up. Dave marches in front of the curtains on the stage. From the wings a follow-spot can be seen to pick out his huge frame. Another huge cheer comes from the audience out front.

DAVE

Ladies and gents, and you buggers at the back – we may not be young, we may not be pretty and we may not be reet good, but for one night and one night only, we're here, we're live and we're going for no less than the Full Monty.

INT. BACKSTAGE. NIGHT

GAZ

Sorry, lads. Good luck, eh?

GUY

Go, Lomps.

INT. WORKING MEN'S CLUB. NIGHT

Lomper leaps on stage, cornet to his lips and plays the first bars of the opening number 'You Can Keep Your Hat On'. Out in the audience, three Old Men – Lomper's pals from the brass band – stand up and belt out the harmony. Lomper raises his cornet in a delighted salute as the curtain goes up to an immense cheer, revealing the Gang in their security guard outfits. Still without Gaz, they go into their routine. The crowd are ecstatic. At the sight of Dave on stage, Bee and Sharon turn to Jean, screaming in delighted

surprise. Jean just grins back proudly. Even the gang of Police who arrested some of them are cheering away at the back. Only Mandy remains unmoved as she cranes her head looking for Gaz.

INT. BACKSTAGE. NIGHT

> NATHAN
> (*distraught*)
> Dad, you can't miss it. Not after everything . . .

> GAZ
> Your Mum's right. I'm no good, kid. At owt.

> NATHAN
> Listen, I'm going to get really annoyed with you in a minute. They're cheering. You did that. Now get out there and do your stuff.

> GAZ
> (*aggrieved*)
> God, is there anyone I don't get bollocked by?

> NATHAN
> (*pointing to the stage*)
> Out.

Gaz raises his eyes in despair, rams his security guard hat on his head and runs for the stage.

> Dad? Thumbs up, eh?

Gaz gives Nathan the thumbs up and dives onto the stage.

INT. ONSTAGE. NIGHT

The biggest roar yet goes up from the crowd as Gaz appears and synchronises perfectly with the Gang. Mandy puts her hand to her face in simultaneous delight and horror. The Police, recognising the ring-leader, roar their approval. Genuine triumph is written on the Gang's faces. Gaz glances into the wings where Nathan is dancing through the moves on his own. They catch each other's eye and smile as the whole Gang go into a final, full-frontal, show-stopping, naked star-jump.

FREEZE FRAME.

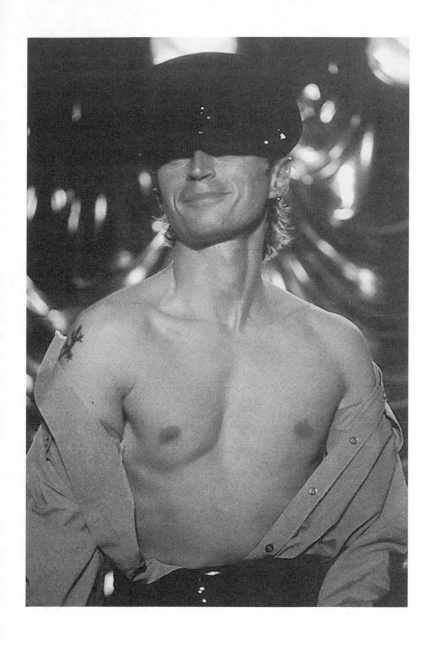

CREDITS

Casting by	SUSIE FIGGIS
Music Composed, Orchestrated and Conducted by	ANNE DUDLEY
Co-producers	POLLY LEYS
	PAUL BUCKNOR
Costume Designer	JILL TAYLOR
Production Designer	MAX GOTTLIEB
Editors	NICK MOORE
	DAVID FREEMAN
Director of Photography	JOHN DE BORMAN B.S.C.
Associate Producer	LESLEY STEWART
Written by	SIMON BEAUFOY
Produced by	UBERTO PASOLINI
Directed by	PETER CATTANEO
First Assistant Director	DAVID GILCHRIST
Script Supervisor	CATHY DOUBLEDAY
Location Manager	ROBERT HOW
Accountant	SUSANNA WYATT
Camera Operator	DAVID WORLEY
Sound Recordist	ALISTAIR CROCKER
Gaffer	TED READ
Make-Up/Hair Designer	CHRIS BLUNDELL
Art Director	CHRIS ROOPE
Second Unit Photography	PETER SINCLAIR
Production Co-ordinator	KATE LEDGER
Production Secretary	SUZANNE FACENFIELD
Production Runners	GAVIN RICKETTS
	DARREN SPENCER
Second Assistant Director	CLAIRE HUGHES
Third Assistant Director	BEN JOHNSON
Floor Runners	SUZANNE LYNCH
	OLIVIA MONTI
	JON WILSON
	JENNIFER WOODS
Stand-ins	JUAN J. J. FALERO
	VICKY NOTTINGHAM

Extras Casting	CAROLE CRANE
	JOCELYN CAMMACK
Locations Assistant	SARAH TAPSFIELD
Assistant Accountant	LYNNE GREENSHIELDS
Focus Puller	BAZ IRVINE
Clapper Loader	KIRSTEN MCMAHON
Camera Trainee	PETER BATESON
Stills Photographer	TOM HILTON
Sound Maintenance Engineer	EDDIE DOUGALL
Sound Trainee	MICHAEL BOTTOMLEY
Best Boy	GEOFF READ
Electricians	JIMMY BRADSHAW
	ROSS CHAPMAN
	VINNY COWPER
	TONY DIFFLEY
Grip	ROBIN A. STONE
Second Grip	PETER SCORAH
Steadicam	SIMON BRAY
	PETER CAVACIUTI
Assistant Make-Up	MARESE LANGAN
Make-Up Trainee	LUCY BENNETT
Assistant Costume Designer	TESSA PHILLIPS
Wardrobe Assistant	NIKITA RAE
Assistant Art Director	EMMA DIBB
Production Buyer	DUNCAN W. WHEELER
Property Masters	JOHN MILLS
	TERRY WOODS
Prop Man	STEVE PUTTOCK
Stand-by Props	GUS LUPTON
Construction Manager	MIKE HOUSEMAN
Carpenter	PAUL FOGERTY
Painter	MARK ADAMS
Stand-by Carpenter	LEON MCCARTHY
Rigger	ALAN STOYLES
Special Effects	IAN ROWLEY
Choreographer	SUZANNE GRAND
Chaperone	JENNY SNAPE
Tutor	PHILLIP HOPPNER

First Assistant Editor	GABRIELLE SMITH
Second Assistant Editors	JATINDERPAL CHOHAN
	CELIA HAINING
	BEN YEATES
	GILES GARDNER
Sound Editor	IAN WILSON
Dialogue and ADR Editor	STEWART HENDERSON
Re-recording	ADRIAN RHODES
Re-recording Assistant	TORIN BROWN
Re-recorded at	DE LANE LEA SOUND CENTRE
Music Editor	GRAHAM LAWRENCE
Foley Artists	JACK STEW
	FELICITY COTTRELL
Foley/ADR Re-recording	TED SWANSCOTT
Music Recorded at	CTS STUDIOS, WEMBLEY and
	ANGEL RECORDING STUDIOS,
	ISLINGTON
Recording Engineers	CHRIS DIBBLE
	STEVE PRICE
Assistant Recording Engineers	NIALL ACOTT
	ERIK JORDAN
Orchestral Recording supervised by	KAREN ELLIOTT
	AIR-EDEL
	ASSOCIATES LIMITED
Harmonica	JULIAN JACKSON
Acoustic Guitar	HUGH BURNS
Musicians Contractor	ISOBEL GRIFFITHS
Music Consultant	LIZ GALLACHER
Publicity	CORBETT & KEENE
Unit Publicist	VIKKI LUYA
Voice Coach	JULIA WILSON-DIXON
Winnebago Drivers	GORDON VICKERS
	RON GREEN
Dining Bus Driver	JOHN DEMPSEY
Wardrobe Vehicle Driver	JEFF EDWARDS
Road Train & Make-up Driver	COLIN STEPHENSON
Caterers	BRENDAN DIVER
	TONY FLAHERTY
	NICKY AGNEW

Licensed by Shapiro Bernstein & Co Ltd., London
Courtesy of Polydor International
Licensed by kind permission from the
Polygram Commerical Marketing Division

'LAND OF A THOUSAND DANCES'
Composed by Chris Kenner
Performed by Wilson Pickett
Published by Longitude Music Co.
Courtesy of Atlantic Recording Corp.
Reproduced by kind permission of Burton Way Music Ltd.
and Rondor Music (London) Ltd.
By arrangement with Warner Special Products

'FLASHDANCE (WHAT A FEELING) '95'
Written by Giorgio Moroder, Irene Cara & Keith Forsey
Recorded by Irene Cara
© Intersong USA Inc./Famous Music Corp./
Giorgio Moroder Publishing Company
Courtesy of Ocean Deep Ltd.
Licensed by kind permission of
Warner/Chappell Music Limited
and from the
Polygram Commercial Marketing Division

'THE STRIPPER'
Written by David Rose
Performed by Joe Loss & His Orchestra
© David Rose Publishing
Courtesy of EMI Records
By kind permission of Warner/Chappell Music Limited
and EMI Special Markets UK

'MAKE ME SMILE (COME UP AND SEE ME)'
Written by Steve Harley
Performed by Steve Harley & Cockney Rebel
© 1975 Trigram/RAK Publishing Limited
Courtesy of EMI Records
By arrangement with EMI Special Markets UK

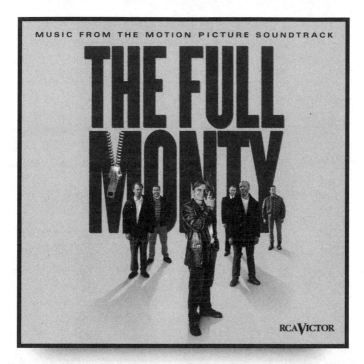